WHAT THE **BIBLE** TEACHES ABOUT

BEING BORN AGAIN

WHAT
THE **BIBLE**
TEACHES
ABOUT

BEING BORN AGAIN

Gary Brady

EVANGELICAL PRESS

EVANGELICAL PRESS
Faverdale North, Darlington, DL3 0PH, England

e-mail: sales@evangelicalpress.org

Evangelical Press USA
P. O. Box 825, Webster, New York 14580, USA

e-mail: usa.sales@evangelicalpress.org

web: http://www.evangelicalpress.org

First published 2008

British Library Cataloguing in Publication Data available

ISBN-13   978-0-85234-674-7   ISBN 0-85234-674-3

Printed and bound in the United States of America.

To all members and friends
of the church meeting at Childs Hill
past, present and future
with thankfulness to God for his goodness.

Contents

Preface 9

Introduction 13

1. What is it exactly? 17

2. What else is true of it? 30

3. What is it not? 43

4. How is it pictured? 56

5. How else is it pictured? 66

6. Why is it necessary? 75

7. What brings it about? 91

8. When does it happen? 102

9. How can you tell it has happened? 117

10. Where does it fit in? 130

11. What are its cosmic dimensions? 143

12. A final plea 149

Appendix 1 163

Appendix 2 167

Select bibliography 173

Preface

In April 1972 I was nearly thirteen and living with my parents in a town called Cwmbran in South Wales. I have reason to believe that it was around this time that I was born again. That event has radically changed the whole of the rest of my life and is one of the major reasons for this present little book.

More immediately, the book had its genesis in some words I read one Monday morning about two years ago as I enjoyed a mid-morning coffee at Brent Cross Shopping Centre here in north-west London. In chapter 2 of *The Old Evangelicalism, old truths for a new awakening,* 'Spurgeon and true conversion' (Banner of Truth, 2005), Iain Murray calls attention to 'the multiplicity of titles on almost all aspects of Christian belief' and the fact that so few are 'on the biblical teaching of conversion' (p. 41). He accuses contemporary evangelical literature of moving what is central in the New Testament to the periphery.

Whether his accusation is fair or unfair, the need to be better acquainted with the unfathomable subject of conversion cannot be denied. We dare not think of regeneration as a mere preliminary to the Christian faith, something that need not long detain our attention. We need to see, as C. H. Spurgeon and others certainly did see, its central importance.

We confess that the present effort is a rather modest, elementary and derivative contribution. We trust, however, that its size (especially compared to previous offerings) and style does not suggest a superficial treatment. We have thought long and hard on the subject for many years and endeavoured to read as many authors as possible before putting the study together in its present form. We trust the many names mentioned will not be off-putting. We are simply seeking to acknowledge some of the sources for the ideas expressed.

Unlike a commentary where the ground to be covered is fairly obvious, this work is more in the area of systematic theology and simply establishing the ground to be covered has been an issue in itself. For help in this and in much else I am very thankful not only to authors mentioned in the text and acknowledged in the bibliography (some read online, some in more conventional ways) but also to various men I have heard preach or lecture on this wonderful subject or with whom I have discussed the sometimes vexed issues over the years.

The systematic nature of the treatment has perhaps made the book a little less interactive than previous works. I am very grateful, however, to the select group who attended the midweek meeting at Childs Hill Baptist Church in autumn 2006 for once again being willing guinea pigs for most of the material.

Colleagues in the ministry, friends at LTS and the John Owen Centre, the Evangelical Library and others have kindly suggested titles and provided books on the subject.

Evangelical Press has again been a great help, especially the anonymous reader who enthusiastically went through the text helping me to reshape my ideas in various ways. I am very grateful for such input.

The worldwide web continues to grow and provided several helpful items. 'Monergism.com' was particularly useful. At one point the hard drive on my old computer malfunctioned after the bulk of the work was complete and I was left reluctantly contemplating the thought of starting again from scratch. A very big thank you, then, to my friends Seyi Olusanya and Gün Kasapoglu for rescuing me!

In the latter stages of the project I have moved on to what is now, I think, my fifth computer. I have been discovering the delights of Open Office, using i-tunes for music to relax to and endeavouring not to be distracted by my penchant for blogging.

As ever, my family and friends have provided help, encouragement and a great deal more. During the course of preparing the book the family enjoyed some very special holidays, thanks to the generosity of my father and various other individuals to whom we are so thankful. What a delight those times were, as are all our times together. As Jesus foretold, we are in some respects a divided family — some are born again, some are not. I trust that this book will help those who are regenerate to understand what God has done more clearly and that it will be a means under God to bring others to the point of spiritual rebirth.

What the Bible teaches about being born again

This year is my twenty-fifth in the ministry. For nearly half my life I have been pastor at Childs Hill Baptist Church in London. These have been happy if sometimes frustrating years. The book is dedicated to all the members and friends who have been involved with us in the past, at present and, God willing, in the future. May God bless you all.

May all who read these pages gain something from them and especially may those of you who are not born again soon come to be so.

Gary Brady
April 2008

Introduction

In many parts of the world today you will meet people who say they are 'born-again Christians'. Numerous individuals claim to be 'reborn' or 'regenerate'. Perhaps you are one of them. Or maybe you have met such people or read about them. Every so often, the media report that some celebrity or other has been 'born again'. Pollsters suggest that as many as eighty to ninety million Americans claim to be born again.

The great eighteenth-century evangelist George Whitefield once wrote to his friend Benjamin Franklin:

> As you have made a pretty considerable progress in the mysteries of electricity, I would now honestly recommend to your diligent unprejudiced pursuit and study the mysteries of the new birth.

This little book is written with the intention of helping those who want to study the subject from a biblical point of view.

If, as we believe, the new birth is what Whitefield's Baptist contemporary Benjamin Beddome describes as 'sinners, dead in trespasses and sins' being 'made alive to God'; 'darkness' being made 'light in the Lord'; 'a child of wrath' becoming 'a child of God', an 'heir of the kingdom'; if it is entering 'a new world, a new state of existence', with 'a new capacity for action' — then it is something we all need to know about and something we all need to understand clearly, whether we have experienced it or not.

Beddome begins a sermon on the subject by saying that 'No subject in religion is of greater importance than that of the new birth.' The Old Princeton theologian Archibald Alexander agreed: 'There is no more important event which occurs in our world.' As Beddome points out, however, errors are frequent and so coming to a right understanding of the subject is not always easy.

In this book, then, we begin with two positive chapters looking at the subject in general, followed by a third that will do the negative work of pointing out the many misconceptions regarding the subject.

We will then go on, in the next two chapters, to fill in the biblical background before tackling a series of six important questions about regeneration: why it is necessary, what brings it about, when it happens, how you can tell it has happened, where it fits in theologically, and what are its cosmic dimensions. The last chapter is given over to a final plea to all readers to act on what has been written.

If you are born again, it is our sincere prayer that what you find here will help you to grow in your understanding of this great change that you have experienced.

Introduction

If you are not born again, we could desire nothing better for you than that you should not only come to understand the subject but be yourself born of God.

If you are unsure of whether you are regenerate or not, it is our purpose to explain the biblical teaching on the subject in such a way that you will no longer be in any doubt about where you stand. More than that, if you discover that you have not experienced new birth, it is our hope and prayer that you will know it, even as you peruse these pages.

We encourage you to read, then, with a prayerful and teachable spirit. May God open your eyes to see wonderful things out of his law.

1.
What is it exactly?

'…you knit me together in my mother's womb … I am fearfully and wonderfully made … My frame was not hidden from you when I was made in the secret place'
(Psalm 139:13-15).

We begin with some brief definitions of biblical new birth and a comparison with natural birth, and will then highlight some leading traits of the 'new birth' — its mystery and profundity, reality and internality, secrecy and perceptibility, and how it changes a man's nature.

The New Testament speaks often enough about the new birth, particularly in the classic passage in John chapter 3. We will say more about this later on but in that chapter, Jesus tells a leading Jewish rabbi called Nicodemus that, just like everyone else, he needs regeneration: he needs to be 'born again'. Nicodemus is well acquainted with religious matters but he does not understand this talk about new birth. 'How can a man be born when he is old?' 'Surely', he argues, 'he cannot enter a second time into his mother's womb to be born!' In other words, what does 'born again' mean? What *is* regeneration? Until that historic meeting, no one had used the phrase in quite the way Jesus did and Nicodemus's confusion is understandable in part. As a Jewish teacher, however, he should have realized what it was all about.

Because of John 3 and similar passages in the Bible, the terms 'born again' and 'regeneration' are sometimes quite popular in certain circles. Not only Christians but others too latch onto such language and use it. In the world of popular music the words 'born again' have featured in the titles of albums and songs by Alice in chains, Black Sabbath, Glenn Frey, Randy Newman and others. *Born again* was also the title of a series of Marvel comic books. A book appeared in the eighties called *The 30 day way to a born again body* and a movement in America promoting celibacy likes to talk of 'born-again virgins'.

These days, even if a celebrity gets a new haircut, it can elicit headlines saying she has been 'reborn'. A witty example of usage would be the tribute band Bjorn Again, who perform songs by Swedish pop group ABBA.

Consciously or unconsciously, such people are borrowing from the Bible without necessarily understanding anything about its teaching. At the same time, even among professed Christians, there can be a good deal of ignorance and misinformation and some definition is necessary.

We want to begin, then, by asking what, according to the Bible, regeneration or new birth is.

Some definitions

Here are some brief, one-sentence definitions based on Scripture. The first is by the Puritan Thomas Watson, the other two by contemporary theologians Wayne Grudem and Jim Packer.

- A supernatural work of God's Spirit, renewing and transforming the heart into the divine likeness.

- A secret act of God in which he imparts new spiritual life to us.

- An inner re-creating of fallen human nature by the gracious sovereign action of the Holy Spirit.

At greater length, Southern Baptist pastor Bill Ascol and Presbyterian scholar Edward Gross call it:

A supernatural work of the Holy Spirit of God which is performed in the life of a sinner whereby the sinner is given a new heart, being brought from spiritual death to spiritual life, and is made able and willing to repent of his sin before God and trust alone in Jesus Christ to be his Lord and Saviour.

The birth by which the new creation of God is begun in the soul. It is the first personal act of rescue wrought by God in us to fulfil his plan of salvation effected by the life, death, and resurrection of Jesus Christ.

> To be a Christian, in the New Testament sense, there has to be a real change of heart within, a new birth.

'Without regeneration,' says Gross, 'we would forever remain spiritually blind and dead.'

Back in the nineteenth century, Anglican Bishop J. C. Ryle wrote of 'that change of heart and nature which a man goes through when he becomes a true Christian'. He calls regeneration the distinguishing mark of the true believer. Being a Christian is more than merely saying you are one. The phrase 'born-again Christian' is really tautology (saying the same thing in two different ways). To be a Christian, in the New Testament sense, there has to be a real change of heart within, a new birth.

Certain aspects of becoming a Christian involve our co-operation but regeneration itself is something that God does alone. The twentieth-century theologian Edwin H. Palmer wrote correctly that 'In regeneration man is 100% passive, and the Holy Spirit is 100% active.' Theologians speak of it as a divinely *monergistic* work. It is the work (Greek *ergon*) of only one (Greek *mono*) — God himself.

To quote Jesus:

No one can come to me unless the Father who sent me draws him, and I will raise him up at the last day. It is written in the Prophets: 'They will all be taught by God. Everyone who listens to the Father and learns from him comes to me'

(John 6:44-45).

Birth and new birth

Back in 1721 in his *Human Nature in its fourfold state*, the Scottish Puritan Thomas Boston drew parallels with physical birth to bring out several aspects of what new birth involves. He spoke of both as being mysterious and how in each case 'the creature comes to a being it had not before'. In both cases the child is passive and there is 'a wonderful contexture of parts' or design, in both. The psalmist says of his earthly body, 'I am fearfully and wonderfully made' (Psalm 139:14). In a similar way, new birth leads to our being 'created to be like God in true righteousness and holiness' (Ephesians 4:24). Boston goes on to note that in both cases, it all 'has its rise from that which is in itself very small and inconsiderable'.

He then says that just as natural generation is carried on by degrees so is regeneration, but here he is thinking of the preparation of the soul for 'quickening' or new birth. Regeneration in its narrower sense is instant. We know that birth is a nine-month affair. When we speak of regeneration in the narrower sense, however, it is not the gestation period that is in view but the event of birth itself. The parallels between gestation and preparation for spiritual quickening are obvious but in regeneration, conception and birth coalesce, as it were, and are the real focus.

Boston draws attention to three other things — new relations, likeness between father and child, and the pain involved. The regenerate are 'born of God'. He is their Father (1 Peter 1:3). There is a sense in which the church is also their mother but that is not part of regeneration. In new birth, we gain a whole family of new brothers and sisters. As participators in the divine nature (2 Peter 1:4) there is a sense in which we resemble our Father. The pain associated with physical birth parallels the cutting to the heart that accompanies true conviction.

We are not to be complacent about salvation, yet we must recognize that only God can regenerate.

Being born again is itself a change that God brings about then, apart from us. The very word regeneration suggests we are passive. Yet when we say *passive*, we must be clear about what that means. We are not to be complacent about salvation, yet we must recognize that only God can regenerate. In regeneration our wills are not destroyed but they yield to a higher will. The nineteenth-century Southern Baptist B. H. Carroll once wrote that the sinner is passive in regeneration:

But he is not a subject of the new birth without contrition [i.e. being sorry], repentance and faith. In exercising these he is active.

Regeneration involves a great change then. We can describe that change using several terms. We will look at four in this chapter and five in the next.

A mysterious and unfathomable change

The new birth is inscrutable and inexplicable. In one of his *Farm sermons* Spurgeon says, 'Regeneration is a great mystery, it is out of your reach ... What can you and I do in this matter? It is far beyond our line.'

This truth is suggested when the Lord says,

'The wind blows wherever it pleases. You hear its sound, but you cannot tell where it comes from or where it is going. So it is with everyone born of the Spirit'

(John 3:8).

Mark 4:27 points in the same direction: 'The seed sprouts and grows, though he does not know how.'

God changes people's hearts. He 'removes from them their heart of stone' and substitutes a heart of flesh (Ezekiel 11:19; 36:26). He enables people to be transformed by the renewing of their minds or to renew the attitude of their minds (Romans 12:2; Ephesians 4:23), which are by nature against God. He introduces a living principle of grace, a holy disposition that makes the soul oppose sin and inclines it to delight in God and divine things.

How exactly he does all this is a great mystery, as Ecclesiastes 11:5 reminds us. Jesus probably had this verse in mind when he spoke to Nicodemus as he did:

As you do not know the path of the wind, or how the body is formed in a mother's womb, so you cannot understand the work of God, the Maker of all things.

The English novelist and critic Anthony Burgess has written of how 'The world was once all miracle. Then everything started to be explained in time. It's only a matter of waiting.'

23

Despite his rueful optimism, what we find is something more complex. Men certainly are rolling back the frontiers of knowledge on various fronts. As time goes by, we understand some things about this universe better and better. Yet, at the same time, we find ourselves growing increasingly aware of just how mysterious and incomprehensible many things are at root. However well we are able to explain how a brown cow eating green grass produces white milk, or how taking some of your food and burying it in the ground means more food in the future, many mysteries yet remain and will remain.

When it comes to theology and the new birth in particular, we should delve into the subject as deeply as we can. However, in the end, we must recognize that it will defy us.

> ...the things revealed belong to us and to our children for ever, that we may follow all the words of this law [but] the secret things belong to the Lord our God
> (Deuteronomy 29:29).

We will never completely understand how God can make a spiritually dead person a new creation or how he can remove his heart of stone and give him a heart of flesh. There is something impenetrable here. We hardly understand the miracle of birth, let alone that of new birth! At some point, we simply have to stand back and cry with Paul,

> Oh, the depth of the riches of the wisdom and knowledge of God! How unsearchable his judgements, and his paths beyond tracing out!
> (Romans 11:33)

Or with Job (5:9; 9:10):

> He performs wonders that cannot be fathomed, miracles
> that cannot be counted.

We cannot 'fathom the mysteries of God' or 'probe the limits
of the Almighty' (11:7-9).

> They are higher than the heavens — what can you do?
> They are deeper than the depths of the grave — what
> can you know? Their measure is longer than the earth
> and wider than the sea.

This includes the new birth.

Imagine an Israelite in the desert who had been bitten by a
venomous snake thinking, 'How can looking at a model of a
bronze snake lifted up heal me?' It seems illogical. Yet 'when
anyone was bitten by a snake and looked at the bronze snake,
he lived' (Numbers 21:9). Similarly, everyone who is born
again and looks by faith to the Son of Man lifted up on the
cross has eternal life. What a mystery!

A real and inward change

Justification brings about a legal or forensic change noted in
the courts of heaven. Regeneration brings about a real, inward
change here on earth. A person's whole nature changes as
God transforms the wayward, worldly and wicked qualities a
man is born with so that he becomes submissive, spiritual and

25

sanctified. This is obvious from the way the Bible speaks of new birth. Writing to Christians in Colosse, Paul says, 'You have taken off your old self with its practices and have put on the new self, which is being renewed in knowledge in the image of its Creator' (Colossians 3:9-10). His words in Titus 3:3-7 and Ephesians 2:1-7 suggest the same thing.

The new birth has really changed thousands and millions of men, women and children. Sometimes the most unlikely and unpromising characters, even murderers and other criminals, have been transformed. Their lives bear strong testimony to the reality of regeneration. People can make a false claim to having been born again, of course, but when it genuinely occurs, the change is real.

A secret but discernible change

Physical birth itself has a secret character. In Psalm 139:15 the writer speaks of how none but God saw him when he was 'made in the secret place' and 'woven together in the depths of the earth'. Something similar is true of the hidden, invisible work of regeneration. It takes place, if we can use the word, in the subconscious and is not directly perceived by the soul.

The change is secret and inward yet not something that can remain concealed. Some dispute this, but the change is usually obvious to the person to whom it has happened. Certainly, from what we have said, it is clear that, ordinarily, an individual to whom it has happened cannot remain ignorant of this great change indefinitely.

The change is also obvious to others. On the basis of evident new birth, New Testament Christians were baptized and accepted as church members. Many churches still endeavour to baptize and receive into membership on this basis today. Even unbelievers see the change to some extent and that is why they often hate and persecute those who have known the second birth.

> The change is secret and inward yet not something that can remain concealed.

These changes are, of course, the immediate results of regeneration rather than the new birth itself. We see the effects, but it is the Spirit, the wind, that is the cause. The results are like fruits on the tree, not the seed in the ground. We see the fruit but the tree's nature dictates the sort of fruit that grows. When a person is born again we see changes because of the renewing of the man's nature.

A quality or nature change

The great American preacher Jonathan Edwards' favourite theological work was a Latin tome that first appeared in 1669. It was by a relatively obscure Dutch theologian called Peter Van Mastricht. Van Mastricht writes of the new birth as:

> a physical operation of the Holy Ghost whereby He begets in men who are elected, redeemed and externally called the first act or principle of spiritual life, by which

they are enabled to receive the offered Redeemer, and comply with the conditions of salvation.

By 'physical operation' he does not mean a *bodily* change. It is not a chemical reaction or a mere change of thinking either. It is a change in a person's 'nature'.

When a person is born again his bodily and mental constitution, the parts of his body and the faculties of his mind, do not materially alter. They are as before. He looks the same, weighs the same. He knows the same things.

New birth can lead to physical effects, especially if a person has been abusing his body with alcohol or other drugs in the past. The change that new birth brings about, however, is the renewal of the *soul*'s main principle.

Dr Gross says, '…the same soul exists, but differently. The same will is there, but with a new, spiritual component.' It is not merely a moral change, the result of advice or warning but 'an altogether new taste for the loveliness of spiritual things' especially as they are taught in the Bible and 'personified by God's Son'. Theologian A. H. Strong used the word *taste*, meaning 'the direction of man's love, the bent of his affections, the trend of his will'. To adapt a Puritan illustration, it is not that the guitar is replaced but that its strings are retuned so that it may play God's melodies. The same eyes are there but they are no longer blind, the same ears but they can now hear.

In his *Treatise concerning religious affections*, Edwards himself helpfully explains that no new faculty of, say, understanding or will is introduced. Rather, new foundations are laid in the nature of the soul for a new kind of exercise of the same faculties. Boston distinguishes the soul's *quality* and *substance*. In the new birth vicious qualities are removed to be replaced by good ones.

The Dutch theologian Abraham Kuyper later used the terms *being* and *nature*, saying the former changes but not the latter. Think of a diesel-powered car. There is the car itself — engine, wheels, bodywork. Then there is its propulsion, once the right fuel is introduced. The former is like *being*, the latter like *nature*. Regeneration leaves the soul's *substance* or *being*, one's 'persona' we might say, the same. However, its *quality* or *nature* is transformed. It moves in a new direction.

Mysterious and unfathomable, real and inward, secret but discernible, a quality or nature change — if you have a proper grasp of the new birth, these characteristics will be at the forefront of your mind when you think about the subject. We will add to the list in the next chapter.

2.
What else is true of it?

*'...you have taken off your old self with its practices
and have put on the new self, which is being renewed in
knowledge in the image of its Creator'*
(Colossians 3:9-10).

Here we highlight five more leading characteristics of biblical regeneration. It is sudden but lasting, vast and deep, miraculous and heavenly, renovating and revolutionary, thorough yet incomplete.

We are considering what regeneration is, according to the Bible. We remind ourselves that, in the words of nineteenth-century American evangelist Asahel Nettleton:

> Of all subjects, that which respects change from death unto life, is certainly one of the most important, and interesting to us. To have clear and definite ideas here is of great moment. Error on such a fundamental point is awfully perilous.

We have said that being born again is something mysterious and unfathomable, real and inward, secret but discernible and a quality or nature change. Here we want to say more.

An instant but eternal change

We cannot always be sure exactly when regeneration has taken place. It is clearly not a gradual thing, however. It is something sudden and instantaneous. The very way the Bible describes new birth suggests this. Spurgeon says,

> Every regeneration is really instantaneous. Its evidences, its outward manifestations may be gradual, but there must be a time when the man begins to live. There must be a period when the first ray of light darts on the opened eye. There must be an instant when the change takes place.

Conversions may be gradual,

> but as to the new birth and the reception of the divine life, there is a distinct line of demarcation — on that side of the line is death, and on this side of it all is life.

Some resist the idea. Opposition often grows out of misunderstanding. To understand regeneration correctly we must keep it distinct in our minds from what leads up to it and what follows. However near to it or far from it a man may be, he is either born again or not born again. The idea of a gradual or progressive regeneration would mean that one could be half-regenerate, half-unregenerate; in a twilight zone, partly in the kingdom, partly outside it; not dead and not alive either; neither new creation nor old.

Such an idea runs contrary to the Bible's teaching. Think not only of the pictures used, which we will examine in the next two chapters, but also of examples like the thief on the cross; the three thousand converted through Peter's preaching on the Day of Pentecost; Cornelius; Lydia; and the Philippian gaoler. These people clearly came to new birth in a moment. One day they were unregenerate, the next they were regenerate.

In his hymn 'Awaked by Sinai's awful sound', the eighteenth-century Native American Samson Occam described how the law was preached and he came to see that 'The sinner must be born again or sink to endless woe.' That fact continued to sound in his ear, torture his mind and even made him sink in despair. Eventually, however, Christ comes and the sinner 'by his grace is born again and sings redeeming love'. Occam is describing something long and drawn out, as conversion can be. Relief, however, when it comes, comes quickly.

Although it is an abrupt change, if it is real, then the new birth produces a lasting change, one that never ends: 'God's seed remains in him' (1 John 3:9); 'The righteous cannot be uprooted' (Proverbs 12:3). God's gifts and call are irrevocable (Romans 11:29). The slogan 'once saved, always saved', though sometimes misused, is appropriate here.

The Puritan Thomas Goodwin wrote of how frozen water can be thawed and even boiled up into steam but it still remains water, liable to freezing again. Corrupt human nature is the same. Unless the divine nature is planted within it, as in the new birth, it will revert to its former self. Once that new birth occurs, however, Christ's victory is certain.

Archibald Alexander notes that if you plant an acorn and it successfully grows then you will not live to see all that will come from that planting. How much more can we say that the consequences of 'the implantation of spiritual life in a soul dead in sin' are without end!

A great and radical change

'A depth-charge in the soul' — that is how one modern writer describes this change. It is something radical and fundamental, a metamorphosis, a transformation. The greatness of the change is apparent when we consider again how the Bible speaks of it. The very idea of new birth, of passing from death to life, of moving from darkness into light, suggests a remarkable reformation. Think of the father's words in the parable of the prodigal: 'For this son of mine was dead and is alive again' (Luke 15:24). That is how radical the change is.

J. C. Ryle said that 'It is as it were to enter upon a new existence.' Thomas Boston used the picture of a fracture specialist. Because man is 'altogether disjointed by the fall … the Lord loosens every joint, and sets it right again'. It is like a woman completely unravelling a woollen scarf in order to re-knit the wool according to an entirely new pattern.

No more profound or far-reaching change can be known than that which brings about new birth.

We speak of a *radical* change because it goes to a person's very core and renews him deep within. No more profound or far-reaching change can be known than that which brings about new birth. Presbyterian pastor Phil Ryken has written: 'It is important to emphasize that the new birth is not simply a new beginning; it is a whole new life.' It is not a make-over. It is not like a change of clothing or even plastic surgery. Rather, you become a new person.

A supernatural and divine change

Alexander observed 'a deep-rooted opinion in the minds of men' that the patent need for reformation and return to God's service 'will be easy whenever they shall determine upon it'. He remarks that 'the need for supernatural power to regenerate the soul is not commonly felt'. When people see how impotent they are, they make their depravity an excuse for not changing. Rather they should look to God for a supernatural change. By supernatural, we mean something beyond unaided human effort.

First, new birth does not come about by natural causes or the operations of nature but by God's immediate power. He alone has the capacity to do it.

Further, it is supernatural in the sense of being beyond man's mutilated and depraved condition by nature. Dr Sinclair Ferguson has written that however we describe new birth, it is a divine activity in men, in which we are *recipients* not actors. This is again clear from Scripture. John 1:13 says the new birth is not down to 'human decision or a husband's will'. It is something God does. He is the one who raises people by grace (Ephesians 2:4-5, 8), as illustrated by the story of the bronze snake lifted up by Moses in the desert; or Paul's conversion as related in the book of Acts.

One old writer rightly says, 'The renovation of the soul, after the image of God, is a work achieved, not by human power and skill but by the great power and energy of the living God.' Puritan George Swinnock likens the preacher to Elisha's servant Gehazi, who was unable to raise the Shunammite's boy (2 Kings 4:8-37). We too have to wait until the Master comes.

Preaching to confederate troops in 1862, the Presbyterian theologian R. L. Dabney noted how the words of Ephesians 1:19-20 exhaust 'the strongest expressions of human language, to assert the divinity and omnipotence of the power by which the sinful soul is changed'. To illustrate, he remarks how a youth may easily pluck a sapling from the ground but when, years later, the sapling is a sturdy tree and the youth 'a worn and tottering old man' it is laughable to think he could uproot it. If he did, we would have to say it was something supernatural. So when we see a sturdy old sinner, 'hardened by half a century of sins', bow to the truth he has so often rejected, it must be the finger of God — his incomparably great power is at work.

In Matthew 19, Jesus meets the rich young ruler and confronts him with the truth. He comments that 'It is easier for a camel to go through the eye of a needle than for a rich man to enter the kingdom of God' (v. 24). The disciples are amazed and ask: 'Who then can be saved?' Jesus' answer is pertinent: 'With man this is impossible, but with God all things are possible.' Regeneration is possible only by a supernatural work of God.

> Regeneration is possible only by a supernatural work of God.

Spurgeon once said that the new creation is as much and entirely a work of God as the old. Augustine said that 'to convert the little world, man, is more than to create the great world'. The Puritan Thomas Watson suggests that this is because there is now opposition to the work and whereas the first creation cost nothing, this new one cost Christ's blood. Furthermore, the first creation took six days while this one happens in a moment.

Preaching on Ephesians 2:5-7 in December 1734, Jonathan Edwards said of regeneration that 'there is more of God in it than in almost any other work'. When we consider that God alone has the power to create (as opposed to merely fashioning) things, then we see that 'new creation' must be his work. Regeneration is a new creation, one that surpasses even the first creation.

In Exodus 4:11 God asks Moses: 'Who gave man his mouth? Who makes him deaf or mute? Who gives him sight or makes him blind? Is it not I, the LORD?' 'Ears that hear and eyes that see,' comments Proverbs 20:12, 'the LORD has made them both.' If this is true in the physical realm, surely it also holds good in the spiritual realm.

Before the Lord's majestic throne,
All nations bow in holy joy;
Know that the Lord is God alone;
He can create, and he destroy.

His sovereign power, without our aid,
Made us of clay, and formed us men;
And though we fell and disobeyed,
He gives us strength to rise again.

As with the resurrection of Christ (Acts 2:24; John 10:17-18; 1 Peter 3:18), there is reason to see spiritual rebirth as a work of Father, Son and Spirit. Calvin speaks of the cause being in the Father, the matter in the Son and the efficacy in the Spirit. Another says, 'as he begat His own son, so he also begets us, so that He is both His and our Father (John 20:17)'. 1 John 5:18 seems to allude to this.

There is also a sense in which it is the work of the Son for he is the believer's life (Galatians 2:20; Colossians 3:4; John 14:6). Phillips Brooks' hymn 'O little town of Bethlehem' ends with the prayer,

O holy child of Bethlehem,
descend to us, we pray;
Cast out our sin and enter in,
be born in us today.

The idea of Emmanuel coming to us and remaining with us is very much what new birth is all about.

In particular we think of regeneration as the Spirit's work. It is 'renewal by the Holy Spirit' (Titus 3:5), a spiritual rebirth (John 3:5). It is the Spirit who gives life (John 6:63).

Among the implications of the divine nature of the second birth are that it is what has been called a sovereign and irresistible work. God regenerates whom he pleases and cannot be refused. Edwards prefers to speak of *efficacious* rather than *irresistible* grace, which he thought 'perfect nonsense' as it simply says that a man can only do what he can do. Grudem points out that it is not that 'people do not make a voluntary, willing choice in responding to the gospel'; rather, it is that 'God's work reaches into our hearts to bring about a response that is absolutely certain.'

A restorative and transforming change

Old Princeton theologian B. B. Warfield used the striking word *repristination* to sum up Paul's way of describing regeneration. The word means 'restoration to an original state'. The soul is made *pristine* or pure again. This alerts us to the fact that new birth involves restoring God's image in us. Christ has come so that his people might also be sons of God:

> And by their second birth regain
> A likeness to his Deity.

The Bible teaches that man was created in God's image or likeness. In the Fall, that likeness was shattered. Death came in and communion with God began to break down. This is the point when Adam first disobeyed God and ate from the tree of the knowledge of good and evil in the Garden of Eden. In the nineteenth century, the American theologians Helfenstein and Witherspoon wrote of regeneration as 'the restoration of God's image to the soul' and 'the reparation of the loss which man sustained by the fall'. A. W. Pink later spoke of a reversal of what happened when Adam sinned and man fell. By means of the new birth God restores us to union and communion with him. Though once dead, the born-again believer is made alive again. He is enabled to cross over from death to life (John 5:24).

Just as spiritual death came about when a principle of evil entered man's being at the Fall, so the spiritual life that being born again brings is the introduction of a new principle of holiness.

God communicates a new principle, as real and as potent as sin. Divine grace is now imparted. A holy disposition is wrought in the soul. A new temper of spirit is bestowed upon the inner man.

Theologians often understand the image of God in terms of Ephesians 4:23-24, which speaks of believers being 'made new in the attitude of your minds' and putting on 'the new self, created to be like God in true righteousness and holiness'. Colossians 3:10 is parallel and speaks of having 'put on the new self, which is being renewed in knowledge in the image of its Creator'.

New birth then leads to the transformation of a darkened mind, a corrupted heart, a deformed morality, perverted affections, a soul antagonistic to God and a thoroughly miserable state. Reason and conscience regain

> **New birth then leads to the transformation of a darkened mind ... [so that] self-centred alienation from God [is] over.**

control over the passions and appetites. Self-centred alienation from God and the disorder it promotes are over.

A universal but imperfect change

Puritan Stephen Charnock called regeneration 'a universal change of the whole man ... as large in renewing as sin was in defacing'. It is, according to Swinnock, a plaster big enough to cover the sore, a sun that travels through all twelve houses of the zodiac.

We must never think of new birth as something partial. Just as man is *totally* depraved by nature, meaning that every part is tainted (sin affects every element in man), so, when he is renewed, he is renewed entirely. There is a total renaissance.

As his mind, will, emotions, conscience and heart are all fallen, so they all need renewing. This is again the import of the Bible pictures. Think, for example, of the idea of 'new creation' (2 Corinthians 5:7). There is a change in the understanding, will, affections and, in consequence, in the person's whole life and conduct. The yeast works through the whole batch of dough. The change is systemic.

The soul is a unit anyway and the idea of God transforming one part while other parts remain hermetically sealed from change makes no sense. As the understanding is illuminated so the affections are excited and the closed heart opens and the hard heart softens. The will is won over too. It is no longer dead but alive, no longer bad but good, no longer stubborn but obedient. Luther described it as 'being changed and sweetly breathed on by the Spirit of God' so that it acts responsively and not by compulsion.

Thomas Boston follows the Puritan approach and highlights several elements in the change. First, the window of the mind or understanding is opened. It is savingly enlightened so that it begins to know about God, sin, self, Christ, the world's emptiness and whatever is spiritual. Second, the will is renewed. It is cured of its inability to will good, given a fixed aversion to evil and inclined to what is good. Third, the emotions are rectified and regulated so that God becomes all and everything. Further, conscience is renewed, memory improved (see John 14:26) and even the body, now the temple of the Spirit, is affected as gracious change shines forth and the person changes his company and becomes a new man in his various relationships and in how he goes about things. There is a new concern for the advancement of God's kingdom and both his use of 'lawful comforts' and his 'performance of religious duties' is transformed.

In the eighteenth century Hannah Moore wrote similarly of a dark understanding illuminated, a rebellious will subdued, irregular desires rectified; judgement informed, imagination chastised, inclinations sanctified, hopes and fears directed to their true and adequate end. The whole internal frame and constitution receive a nobler bent, she says — the mind's intents and purposes, a sublimer aim; aspirations, a loftier flight; vacillating desires, a fixed object; vagrant purposes, a settled home; a disappointed heart, a certain refuge.

Unconverted people who are interested in Christianity will sometimes ask what they have to give up to become Christians. Perhaps the best answer to that question is 'everything'. When you are born again, everything changes. Nothing is ever quite the same again. As the seed grows, its tendrils reach out into every nook and cranny. No part of life is exempt.

Finally, for all the positive things we can say about the new birth it is right to remind ourselves that, as Boston notes, it is an imperfect change. Just as a newborn baby is not a mature man, so a newborn Christian has plenty of developing to do. It is important that we do not expect too much. Thomas Watson says, 'The new creature is but begun here; it is not perfected or drawn in all its orient colours till it comes to heaven.' Calvin warns, 'There still remains in a regenerate man a fountain of evil, continually producing irregular desires.' The fight against sin goes on to the end. We should pray with Wesley,

> Finish, then, Thy new creation;
> Pure and spotless may we be.

It is not 'Till in heaven we take our place' that we will know the perfect restoration found in Christ.

Previously we said that new birth is something mysterious and unfathomable, real and inward, secret but discernible and a quality or nature change. We have now added to the description by saying that it is instant but eternal, great and radical, supernatural and divine, restorative and transforming and a universal but imperfect change.

3.
What is it not?

'"How can a man be born when he is old?" Nicodemus asked. "Surely he cannot enter a second time into his mother's womb to be born!"'
(John 3:4).

Here, for the sake of clarity, we list a number of things that should *not* be confused with the biblical idea of being born again, including reincarnation, commitment, baptism, etc.

It is good to accentuate the positive but we ought to make some effort to eliminate confusion and here we want to tie things down with a series of *nots*. We shall therefore list some points that, from a biblical viewpoint, regeneration is *not*.

Not a cross-generational reincarnation

The story is told of a keen young Christian witnessing to his Hindu neighbour. At one point he says to him, 'You see, what needs to happen is that you have to be born again!' The Hindu believes in the transmigration of souls, or metempsychosis, the idea that after death the soul begins a new life in another body, so he answers, 'But, my dear friend, I've been born again many times!' More than one Hindu book aimed at westerners has commended the idea of being born again and again.

The recognition of the need for renewal is good but the theory is riddled with difficulties. Hindus and others sometimes refer to reincarnation as regeneration but when the Bible speaks of it, this is not what it means. Christian regeneration or rebirth is something that occurs in *this* life not in any future one!

Not a continuous process

In 1889 an American couple, Charles and Myrtle Fillmore, founded the Unity Church. Now two million strong, it works in fifteen countries promoting so-called 'practical Christianity'. Among its distinctives is a notion that being born again is a continuous process that needs to be repeated. The idea is clearly attractive to some but, in Scripture, new birth happens once and for all; it is not a process. It is a fountain not a river; the ignition of the engine not its continuous hum; birth not growth.

Not a renewal of the spirit apart from the soul

Another understanding of the new birth we should warn against is one that arises out of the view that man is made up of three parts not two (spirit, soul and body, not just soul and body). It is sometimes assumed that sin resides only in the soul, the spirit remaining pure. Once the soul is renewed, the proper balance is regained and the body will follow suit. Whatever view we take of man's composition (trichotomy, dichotomy; three parts or two), to deny our utter depravity — body, soul, spirit, mind, heart — is a serious mistake and is bound to lead us astray.

Not a material change

Before his conversion, Augustine of Hippo was involved in a religious movement called Manichaeism. It began in Persia in the third century AD and among its teachings, according to later theologians, was the erroneous view that regeneration is a change in substance. Others have held similar views. A sixteenth-century Lutheran called Illyricus taught that in regeneration a substance called original sin is replaced by another substance. In fact, no addition to or subtraction from the soul is involved.

In the seventeenth century, as noted, some Reformed theologians do refer to regeneration as something *physical* but in using this term they were not suggesting there is a material change. Rather, this was their way of referring to a change in nature (*phusis*).

> ...to deny our utter depravity — body, soul, spirit, mind, heart — is a serious mistake and is bound to lead us astray.

Not a simple choice

Back in the second half of the fourth century, there was a monk called Pelagius who initially lived somewhere in the British Isles. He and his followers believed that sin is only a matter of making wrong choices. A man can choose to sin. A man can choose not to sin. Being born again is chiefly a matter of choosing not to sin. It is an 'act of the soul', a mere reformation of life and habit. The person who once chose to break God's law, now chooses to obey it.

Pelagius's sub-biblical form of Christianity was condemned at the Council of Ephesus in AD 431 but later groups have taught similar things. Most common are those who, like Pelagius's contemporary John Cassian, are Semi-Pelagian. In the seventeenth century Jacobus Arminius and his followers (Arminians) blazed a trail in this direction. They accept the need for the Spirit to work but taught that he can be resisted and that regeneration can be lost.

In the nineteenth century, the American evangelist and theologian Charles Finney taught that regeneration is, to quote a sermon of his, 'a voluntary change in the governing preference of the mind, or a change of choice'. More recently, the popular American writer Joyce Meyer has produced a book called *The most important decision you will ever make.* It claims to teach you 'what you must believe to be born again'. The very title of the book suggests an inadequate view of the subject.

The truth is that all sorts of people make a fresh start or a new beginning. Turning over a new leaf can be a good thing as far as it goes, but it is not at all what the Bible means when it talks of regeneration or being born again. We need a far more comprehensive change, a transformation that only new birth can bring about. Our need is not to make a new start in life but to receive a new life to start with.

Charles Naylor put it well, back in 1907:

No mere reformation your sins can erase,
You cannot remove their stain;
If ever in heaven your soul has a place,
You must be born again.

Whitewashing walls is not enough. The whole house needs to be reconstructed.

Not a fresh commitment

Surveys in the USA often reveal a high percentage of individuals claiming to be 'born again'. On further examination, it is evident that many simply mean that at some point, often in their teens, they made some sort of Christian commitment. They went forward at an evangelistic rally, or prayed a prayer of commitment alone or with someone else. They made an emotional response to God in a personal crisis or after watching a religious film, or signed a decision card. Perhaps you have done something similar yourself.

Such acts and responses may accompany Christian conversion but are again not something that we can equate with regeneration. Charles Finney fostered this sort of thinking and many have copied him. The first page of his *Lectures on Revivals* declares, disturbingly, his belief that 'religion is the work of man'. A modern book aimed at teenagers sets out its understanding of the gospel and gives a model prayer to pray. It then says, 'If you sincerely prayed that prayer, you are now born again.' This can only be true if we regard new birth merely as a commitment, rather than taking a biblical view of the subject.

Contemporary Presbyterian theologian Jay E. Adams' booklet *Decisional regeneration* warns against this sort of misunderstanding. He points out that Charlotte Elliott's 1836 hymn 'Just as I am', often used when 'altar calls' are given, was written with invalids in mind. Bedridden herself, Elliott did not equate the words 'I come, I come' with a walk down an aisle or across a sports field; nor should we. The *coming* in mind is the heart's response following its renewal by God.

Not a moving experience

A 1970s love song by David Shire and Carol Connors includes the line, 'Woman, don't you know, with you I'm born again.' On a web site, singer Michael Jackson is quoted describing his conversion to Islam with the words, 'I felt as if I were born again.' It is perhaps this understanding of the term that leads some Mormons, members of the Church of Latter Day Saints, to describe themselves as 'born again'. American novelist Gore Vidal provocatively described himself as 'a born-again atheist' and others have similarly declared themselves 'born-again sceptics' or 'born-again cynics'!

Though people equate being born again with 'feeling brand new' and sometimes speak of falling in love and other emotional upheavals in such terms, when the Bible speaks about being born again it is not speaking about a moving experience.

In 1721, Thomas Boston pointed out how 'a person may have sharp soul-exercises and pangs and yet', as it were, 'die in the birth'. Not all that glitters is gold and spring blossom cannot guarantee summer fruit. Sharp convictions can 'go off'. Awakening grace is not converting grace. Some 'stillborns' (or almost Christians) make the mistake of thinking that having a deep conviction of sin is enough. To receive the Word with joy is not to be born again (Matthew 13:20).

> **Awakening grace is not converting grace.**

People of many different religious backgrounds, and even some with none at all, use regeneration language to describe moving experiences, but this is not what we are talking about here.

Not a change of opinion

Some theologians have seen regeneration as the discovery of one's potential divinity, an ethical change that led to following higher principles. More recently, under post-modern influences, professing evangelicals in the 'emergent church' have been saying similar things. Steve Chalke, for example, seems to understand Christ's call to regeneration simply as a call to see the world differently and adopt a new agenda. It is to discover, he says, the freedom found in God's love and rule. Brian McLaren similarly sees no need for the Holy Spirit to bring it about. Such thinking is unbiblical.

Not a psychological effect

William James, brother of novelist Henry, was a philosopher and psychologist. Like other writers on religious experience, he wanted to dismiss all idea of the new birth being supernatural. He saw it as something psychological occurring in the subconscious, in which a person moves from a self-centred (auto-centric) standpoint to a hetero-centric one, focused elsewhere.

He writes of how a self that has been 'divided, and consciously wrong, inferior and unhappy' becomes 'unified and consciously right, superior and happy, in consequence of its firmer hold on religious realities'. As we have suggested, even some professing Christians hold similar views but this is not what the Bible teaches.

Not a consequence of baptism

Since the post-apostolic period many have taught 'baptismal regeneration' — the spiritual rebirth of a baby at baptism. That a baby *could* be regenerated at the time of baptism is not disputed, but that it happens *because* of baptism is.

Roman Catholicism teaches that baptism not only cancels the guilt of any actual sin and any punishment due as a result of it, but it also removes the power of original (inherited) sin to defile and corrupt. Baptism renews the moral nature and the subject becomes a son and heir of God. It is believed that this happens every time an infant is baptized but that adults can resist baptism's virtue or make it invalid.

Lutherans and Anglicans often see regeneration at baptism as the norm. The Anglican baptismal service says of the baptized baby, 'This child is regenerate.' It has pleased God to 'regenerate the infant'. Some say it is a judgement of charity but others suggest that a germ of spiritual life is planted in the soul that may long remain dormant until it bears fruit or eventually withers and dies.

Some allow for both biblical regeneration and 'baptismal regeneration', which they see as a change in a person's state or relation so that he is in some sense, 'a son of God'. Both acts, they say, are the work of the Spirit.

The *Prayer Book* is a problem for Bible-believing Anglicans. In 1864, C. H. Spurgeon, a Baptist, opposed baptismal regeneration as it was not taught by God and was not found anywhere in the Bible. In the same period, Anglican theologian J. B. Mozley agreed. 'Scripture nowhere asserts, either explicitly or implicitly, the regeneration of infants in baptism,' he wrote.

Others directly connect the water baptism of older people with rebirth in ways the Bible never does. Regardless of vain appeals to 1 Peter 3:21 or John 3:3, baptism is an act of obedience and cannot produce regeneration. Simon Magus was baptized but he was no true convert (see Acts 8). Isaac Watts reminds us:

Not all the outward forms on earth,
Nor rites that God has given,
Nor will of man, nor blood, nor birth,
Can raise a soul to heaven.

Not a result of confirmation or community

In a similar way, some speak of a service of confirmation into the church or of church membership as regeneration. It is true that all who are born again are members of the universal church. Simply joining a local church or having someone's hands laid on your head, however, cannot produce the biblical new birth.

In the nineteenth century German modernist Friedrich Schleiermacher spoke more complexly of regeneration being produced in a person by the common Christian spirit of the community. Again, this is not what Scripture is speaking about when it refers to this matter.

As Boston says, one may be civil and sober and even follow all the outward duties of religion without ever being regenerate. We may be very strict in these things, like Paul the Pharisee, 'yet be strangers to the new birth'.

Not a denominational matter

The ancient Persian religion of Mithraism described initiation into its mysteries as 'regeneration'. In Christianity, there are no hidden mysteries of that sort. All are free to know what we teach. Regeneration cannot, therefore, be anything like this.

'Born-again Christians' can be found in different Christian denominations and groupings. As far as we are aware, there is no 'born-again Christian' denomination, though some churches use the words 'new birth' in their names. Even if there is a 'born-again' denomination, or if one came into existence, regeneration could not be a matter of joining such a group. Simply joining a group or signing up to a confession, whatever its name, cannot of itself regenerate anyone. Churches and creeds do not make Christians.

> ◇◇◇◇◇◇◇◇◇◇◇◇◇◇◇◇◇◇◇◇◇◇◇◇◇◇◇◇◇
> **Simply joining a group or signing up to a confession, whatever its name, cannot of itself regenerate anyone.**
> ◇◇◇◇◇◇◇◇◇◇◇◇◇◇◇◇◇◇◇◇◇◇◇◇◇◇◇◇◇

Not an American thing

Another idea is that 'born-again Christian' is just a phrase that certain American Christians, or rather vocal and enthusiastic Christians elsewhere, like to use. In fact, though Americans have invented many wonderful things, from chewing gum to manned flight, being born again is not one of them.

It is true that the influence of Evangelical and Fundamentalist Christians from the USA is great. It is true that go-getting American attitudes affect Christians as well as others. It is also true that in the seventies there was something of a 'born-again movement' in the USA. In 1976, presidential candidate and later president Jimmy Carter described himself in interviews as 'born again' and Charles Colson, converted Watergate felon, brought out his top-selling autobiography *Born again*. In 1977 American evangelist Billy Graham produced his best-seller *How to be Born Again*.

However, to suggest that being born again is a simple matter of being an American or belonging to a certain movement is unfair and incorrect.

Not a form of justification or conversion

We will look at how regeneration relates to other aspects of salvation later. Here it is worth noting, however, that in the early years after Christ, Christian writers spoke of regeneration in quite general terms. For example, they did not distinguish justification by faith and the new birth. The two are still confused in Roman Catholic thinking today. Over the centuries, others have defined the terms in narrower and more biblical ways, especially since the Reformation.

Augustine grasped the importance of seeing new birth as an irresistible work of God but was not as clear as later writers. With Martin Luther things improved, but even the Reformer John Calvin did not distinguish regeneration from conversion and the ongoing work of sanctification. Later Protestant theologians saw things more clearly, but we often find them lumping conversion and regeneration together.

Today, although some good writers still use the word 'regeneration' to speak of the *effects* of new birth rather than the change itself, the best writers rightly confine terms such as born again and regeneration to the very specific matter of the way God changes a person's heart at the beginning of the Christian life.

Not a simple acceptance of the Bible

Perhaps a final thing to say is that being born again is not a matter of simply believing the Bible. A good Bible knowledge cannot guarantee anything. It is important that we accept the

Bible as God's Word, of course, including what it says on regeneration. However, new birth involves something more than accepting that the Bible is true.

Agreeing with its ethical teachings, as set out in the Ten Commandments or the Sermon on the Mount, is not enough either. Simply conforming to rules and regulations cannot make a person a born-again Christian. As we will see, something more is needed.

To sum up then, regeneration is not a cross-generational reincarnation, a continuous process nor a renewal of the spirit but not the soul. It is not a material change. It is not a simple choice, a fresh commitment, a moving experience, a change of opinion or something psychological. It is not a consequence of baptism, of confirmation or community membership or of joining a certain denomination. It is not an American 'thing' either and we must not confuse it with conversion or justification or a simple acceptance of the Bible.

Whether you yourself are born again or not, if you have thought of regeneration in any of these ways then you need to realize your mistake and repent. Ask the Lord to help you to distinguish biblical new birth from its many counterfeits.

4.
How is it pictured?

'You must be born again'
(John 3:7).

Next we want to explore the main biblical picture of regeneration, being reborn, and give the Old Testament background.

It is true that the exact phrase 'new birth' never occurs in the Bible. It is true that the noun 'regeneration' appears only twice (see Titus 3:5; Matthew 19:28, AV; the NIV translates *renewal*). However, terms such as 'born of God', 'born again', 'new creation', 'new self' and 'new man' are fairly common.

The phrase 'born again' is reasonably self-explanatory, and the Latin-based *regeneration* is similarly obvious. To generate something is to produce or give birth to it. A *generation* can be all the people born in a certain age bracket. 'Re' simply means 'again'.

Plainly, when the Bible speaks in such terms it is using a picture. New birth suggests the beginning of life, entrance into a new world. The images are used in slightly different ways, so it is important to draw our ideas from the Bible itself. Several passages speak about regeneration by using the picture of new birth. As noted, the classic passage that chiefly introduces us to 'born again' language is the Gospel of John, chapter 3.

Jesus and Nicodemus in John 3

The chapter features an encounter between Jesus and a Pharisee named Nicodemus who belonged to the ruling council of the Jews or Sanhedrin. The other three Gospel writers do not mention him; he appears only in John's Gospel. John tells us how Nicodemus later spoke up for Jesus in the ruling council, only to be shouted down (7:50-51). He also reveals how eventually, after the crucifixion, Nicodemus helped Joseph of Arimathea to anoint the dead body of Jesus (19:39). This information suggests that after becoming something of a secret disciple for a while, he acted boldly and publicly for Jesus. At some point after his conversation with Jesus, he himself must have been born again.

John says Nicodemus came to visit Jesus at night. What prompted him to come at night? Was it prudence? Perhaps Jesus was too busy in the day. Was it zeal? Maybe he could not wait until the following day. Was it fear? Did he not want to be seen visiting Jesus? Or was it simply that, like other rabbis, it was his habit to spend the hours of darkness talking and discussing theology?

◇◇◇◇◇◇◇◇◇◇◇◇◇◇◇◇◇◇◇◇◇◇◇◇

...the passage from darkness into light is another way of picturing regeneration.

◇◇◇◇◇◇◇◇◇◇◇◇◇◇◇◇◇◇◇◇◇◇◇◇

Whatever the reason, no doubt John mentions it to underline the fact that darkness was reigning in Nicodemus's heart. John loves the imagery of light and darkness and uses it often (see 5:35; 8:12; 9:5; etc.). When Judas Iscariot leaves the upper room at the Last Supper John says, 'As soon as Judas had taken the bread, he went out. And it was night' (13:30). As we shall see, the passage from darkness into light is another way of picturing regeneration.

Back in John 3, Nicodemus' opening gambit is to say to Jesus, 'Rabbi, we know you are a teacher who has come from God. For no one could perform the miraculous signs you are doing if God were not with him' (v. 2). Jesus does not thank him for this or invite him to be a disciple or pronounce him a Christian. Unwilling to accept this rather roundabout way of discussing things, he instead cuts straight to the chase with a firm, 'I tell you the truth, no one can see the kingdom of God unless he is born again.'

The only miraculous sign John has described so far in his Gospel is the transforming of water into wine (John 2). When the Jews ask Jesus for a miraculous sign to show his authority to cleanse the temple (2:18) he draws attention to his coming resurrection. Nicodemus acknowledges Jesus' miraculous signs but has not yet begun to grasp their significance — the way they point to new life in Christ.

'I tell you the truth' is simply *Amen* in the original, a Hebrew word that we all know, which means, 'It is so'. God's *kingdom* is really his reign. Whether Jesus' emphasis is on the present or future aspects of God's kingdom at this point is not important. The word *again* can be rendered 'from above', though Nicodemus understands it to mean 'once more'. The word for 'born' can refer to a man fathering or a woman bearing a child, although in this instance it relates to a particular event, rather than a process.

We could paraphrase then, 'Amen, I say to you, no one can know God reigning over him unless he starts all over again from the top.' We can only know God's kingdom or rule in our lives if there is a radical change from above akin to becoming a new person. Believing Jesus was sent by God, accepting his miracles — none of this is enough. There must be a 'top to bottom' change. For all his knowledge, gifts, experience, religious zeal and community standing, Nicodemus still needs a total, radical transformation.

It is difficult to gauge the tone of Nicodemus's reaction when he responds, 'How can a man be born when he is old? … Surely he cannot enter a second time into his mother's womb to be born!' Is he offended? Jewish proselytes were sometimes spoken of as 'newborns'. Is Jesus suggesting he is only a beginner? Is Nicodemus being dismissively sarcastic? 'This is impossible!' Is he genuinely incredulous and perplexed? Is he wistful? Does he genuinely long for a fresh start but cannot see how it is possible? Does he simply want to know more?

Whichever it is, Jesus elaborates.

I tell you the truth, no one can enter the kingdom of God unless he is born of water and the Spirit. Flesh gives birth to flesh, but the Spirit gives birth to spirit. You should not be surprised at my saying, 'You must be born again.' The wind blows wherever it pleases. You hear its sound, but you cannot tell where it comes from or where it is going. So it is with everyone born of the Spirit.

The reference to 'water and the Spirit' has prompted much discussion. Some assume a reference to physical then spiritual birth. Others are keen to bring baptism in or try to link it to the role God's Word plays in new birth (see Ephesians 5:26). It is likely that none of these apply. Twentieth-century theologian John Murray, following Calvin, was probably right when, in *Redemption accomplished and applied*, he saw a reference to the double work of cleansing and renewal. This is likely to be the way that Nicodemus understood it. He would have known Ezekiel 36:25-27 where God says to Israel:

I will sprinkle clean water on you, and you will be clean; I will cleanse you from all your impurities and from all your idols. I will give you a new heart and put a new spirit in you; I will remove from you your heart of stone and give you a heart of flesh. And I will put my Spirit in you and move you to follow my decrees and be careful to keep my laws.

It also chimes in with Titus 3:5 where Paul speaks of God saving 'through the washing of rebirth and renewal by the Holy Spirit'. As we shall see, this is the sole use of the picture by Paul, who speaks more about justification. When he refers to regeneration he prefers to use the picture of 'being made alive' or 'becoming a new creation'.

The *washing* here could be a symbol of renewal (baptism) or an effect of renewal. It is most likely that Paul sees washing and renewal as two aspects of the same thing and that is the same thought in John 3:5. In light of Paul's theology, he probably has in mind here not just inward renewal but, according to Sinclair Ferguson, a 'participation in the power of the new age and … with the resurrected Christ…'

The New Testament uses the word 'flesh' in different ways but here in John 3 it is stressing human weakness. The sinful nature itself cannot bring forth something spiritual. It is only the Holy Spirit who can bring about regeneration, which leads to spiritual change. The Spirit gives the individual a new spiritual nature. As Thomas Goodwin puts it: 'The soul of man born again is spiritualised.' All the gracious, heavenly inclinations and characteristics we see in true believers come from the Spirit's work within.

The new birth is impossible for weak humans, but is possible when God the Spirit works. This fact cannot be overemphasized and it is important that we have this clear in our minds. We have seen the point being made in Titus 3:5. A similar point is made in John 1:12-13, where John says that although Jesus was rejected by his people to whom he came,

> Yet to all who received him, to those who believed in his name, he gave the right to become children of God — children born not of natural descent [literally *bloods*], nor of human decision or a husband's will, but born of God.

The fact that receiving or believing appears to arise before becoming children of God or being born of God in these verses tempts some to think that receiving or believing is a *condition* for being born of God. However, the whole point of the passage is that becoming a child of God is not a matter of 'natural descent, nor of human decision or a husband's will'. *God* makes it happen. As Paul observes: 'I planted the seed, Apollos watered it, but God made it grow' (1 Corinthians 3:6). Only God, the giver of life, can make alive. The same point is made in a previous quotation from Ezekiel 36, where God says,

I will give you a new heart and put a new spirit in you; *I* will remove from you your heart of stone and give you a heart of flesh [italics mine].

> Just as birth comes at the beginning of our conscious human life so new birth is at the start of the Christian life.

The *you* in 'you must be born again' (John 3:7) is plural. Everyone needs to be born again, not just Nicodemus. The words are often misunderstood to mean that we must do something ourselves to be born again. Yet the picture itself suggests the very opposite. Grammatically, this is an indicative not an imperative, a statement not a command. Just as we cannot decide to be born, so we cannot decide to be born again. Just as birth comes at the beginning of our conscious human life so new birth is at the start of the Christian life.

Jesus uses a picture that grows out of the fact that in Hebrew, Greek and other languages, the word for Spirit or spirit is also the word for *breath* or *wind*. This is because both are invisible. Just as 'the wind blows wherever it pleases', so the Spirit regenerates whom he will. In the same way that you cannot see the wind but you can see where it has been and what it does, so the Spirit works in people's lives, and though his work is invisible to our eyes the results are seen in changed lives. Just when and where the Spirit will work next we cannot definitely know.

Isaac Watts takes up the image in a hymn:

The Spirit, like some heavenly wind,
Breathes on the sons of flesh,
Creates anew the carnal mind,
And forms the man afresh.

Our quickened souls awake and rise
From their long sleep of death;
On heavenly things we fix our eyes,
And praise employs our breath.

At this point Nicodemus is clearly lost and asks: 'How can this be?' Jesus rebukes him for his ignorance. He is a rabbi. He is supposed to be 'Israel's teacher', yet, like many others in his day, and ours, he does not know these primary truths. If he does not understand the basic earthly teachings how will he understand anything else? He is struggling to get into the school of new birth; what hope of a place in the university of heaven?

Jesus goes on to speak about his incarnation, the cross (which then lay in the future), and the importance of faith in him. He makes clear that this is the basis upon which it is possible for people to be born again.

Old Testament background

As we have said, the idea of new birth is not confined to the New Testament. We noted the reference, in Ezekiel 36, to God taking away the heart of stone and replacing it with a heart of flesh. It is also in Ezekiel 11:19-20, where God says,

> I will give them an undivided heart and put a new spirit in them; I will remove from them their heart of stone and give them a heart of flesh. Then they will follow my decrees and be careful to keep my laws. They will be my people, and I will be their God.

Jeremiah looks forward to the bringing in of the new covenant. God promises (Jeremiah 31:33) to 'put my law in their minds and write it on their hearts. I will be their God, and they will be my people' (see also Jeremiah 32:39).

Back in Deuteronomy 30:6 God speaks in terms of a circumcision of the heart. 'The LORD your God will circumcise your hearts and the hearts of your descendants, so that you may love him with all your heart and with all your soul, and live.' Paul takes this up in the New Testament and says,

> A man is not a Jew if he is only one outwardly, nor is circumcision merely outward and physical. No, a man

is a Jew if he is one inwardly; and circumcision is circumcision of the heart, by the Spirit, not by the written code. Such a man's praise is not from men, but from God.

In him you were also circumcised, in the putting off of the sinful nature, not with a circumcision done by the hands of men but with the circumcision done by Christ (Romans 2:28-29; Colossians 2:11).

In the Bible leprosy, then a living death, can symbolize human sin and so cleansing from it parallels regeneration. Leviticus 14 explains how a healed leper was to observe certain rituals, including washing and shaving his whole body so that he appeared clean and like a newborn baby. As Philip Eveson says in his commentary on the passage, 'It was as if he or she had been born all over again'. As for the question of whether it is right to say that holy people in the Old Testament were regenerate, please see the brief appendix on the subject at the end of this book.

A major way to speak about regeneration then is in terms of being born again. However, there are other pictures — being washed, receiving a new heart or spirit, having God's law in the mind and on the heart, and having the heart circumcised. In each case, we are talking about a major radical and inward change brought about by God.

Finally, with William T. Sleeper, we urge you not to let these words come to you in vain. You must be born again!

O ye who would enter that glorious rest,
And sing with the ransomed the song of the blest,
The life everlasting if you would obtain,
'Ye must be born again'.

5.
How else is it pictured?

'Therefore, if anyone is in Christ, he is a new creation;
the old has gone, the new has come!'
(2 Corinthians 5:17).

'For he has rescued us from the dominion of darkness
and brought us into the kingdom of the Son he loves'
(Colossians 1:13).

This chapter explores other biblical pictures, such as planting and resurrection, that highlight the Bible's teaching about the new birth.

The idea of a fundamental change equal to a new birth is not something confined to one or two chapters of the New Testament. The idea is found in many places and a variety of illustrations are employed.

Born of God

The apostle Peter begins his first letter praising 'the God and Father of our Lord Jesus Christ' who 'in his great mercy … has given us new birth into a living hope through the resurrection of Jesus Christ from the dead' (1 Peter 1:3). In verse 23 he reminds believers that they 'have been born again, not of perishable seed, but of imperishable, through the living and enduring word of God'. The idea of new birth coming through the Word is found also, in a slightly different form, in James 1:18. James uses a word that applies only to a mother giving birth not to a man fathering a child. He says that God 'chose to give us birth through the word of truth, that we might be a kind of firstfruits of all he created'.

However, it is John who seems to have been most prone to using new birth imagery. As well as the references in the Gospel, his first letter contains many uses of the phrase 'born of God' (see 1 John 2:29; 3:9; 4:7; 5:1, 4, 18). We will consider these verses when we look at evidence for the new birth.

1 John 5:1 says that 'Everyone who believes that Jesus is the Christ is born of God.' Like other verses, it may seem at first glance to be teaching that faith comes before regeneration. In fact, it is when a person goes on believing that Jesus is the Christ that we have evidence that he is truly born again.

The planting of seed

In the Sermon on the Mount we find Jesus using words that imply the idea of a fundamental change equal to a new birth.

He says, 'Every good tree bears good fruit, but a bad tree bears bad fruit' (Matthew 7:17). What dictates whether we do good or bad deeds is our nature.

Simply sticking apples onto a tree does not make it an apple tree. If it is going to produce apples, it has to be an apple tree by nature. By nature, the Bible teaches, we are evil and unless there is a fundamental and radical change, we will remain so. The idea is perhaps implicit too in the references in the same chapter to entering 'through the narrow gate' (Matthew 7:13-14).

Using a slightly different picture, Jesus also says that 'Every plant that my heavenly Father has not planted will be pulled up by the roots' (Matthew 15:13). It is when God plants the seed in our hearts that the fruit of good deeds is possible. This idea is also illustrated in the parable of the sower.

> **It is when God plants the seed in our hearts that the fruit of good deeds is possible.**

We have mentioned Peter speaking of being 'born again, not of perishable seed, but of imperishable' (1 Peter 1:23). John speaks of 'God's seed' remaining in the one 'who is born of God' (1 John 3:9). The latter parallel is probably human seed rather than wheat or barley but the idea is similar in some ways to the picture of planting seed in the ground.

Another picture from the world of farming and gardening that probably refers to the new birth is the idea of being grafted into a cultivated olive tree (Romans 11:24).

A new creation

Paul, as we noted, is quite happy to talk about 'the washing of rebirth and renewal by the Holy Spirit' (Titus 3:5). Most often, however, he refers to new birth in terms of being raised to life. Professor Richard Gaffin may be right to caution against the tendency to identify these references too closely with the new birth. Certainly when Paul says that believers have 'been buried with him in baptism and raised with him *through your faith in the power of God*, who raised him from the dead' (Colossians 2:12), he must be referring to the resurrection life believers live by faith rather than an initial resurrection received by faith.

In Ephesians 2, Paul reminds Christian readers that by nature they 'were dead in … transgressions and sins' (2:1) but in his mercy God has made them 'alive with Christ even when … dead in transgressions' (2:5). (Colossians 2:13 is parallel: 'When you were dead in your sins and in the uncircumcision of your sinful nature, God made you alive with Christ'; see also Romans 4:17.) The same power that God 'exerted in Christ when he raised him from the dead and seated him at his right hand in the heavenly realms' (1:19-20) is the power now at work in regenerate sinners. Believers have been newly 'created in Christ Jesus to do good works, which God prepared in advance for us to do' (2:10).

The Puritan Stephen Charnock once wrote that,

There is as real a resurrection of the soul, by the trumpet of the gospel, accompanied with the vigorous efficacy of the Holy Ghost, as there shall be of bodies by the voice of the Son of God, at the sound of the trumpet of the archangel.

Christians 'have been brought from death to life' (Romans 6:13). Jesus spoke in similar terms in John 5:21:

> For just as the Father raises the dead and gives them life, even so the Son gives life to whom he is pleased to give it.

In his first letter, John picks this up and says that as believers 'we have passed from death to life' (1 John 3:14).

Elsewhere, Paul speaks of being in Christ as being 'a new creation; the old has gone, the new has come!' (2 Corinthians 5:17). Hence his important remark, 'Neither circumcision nor uncircumcision means anything; what counts is a new creation' (Galatians 6:15). The believer must live a holy life precisely because of this amazing change.

If you are a believer you have 'taken off your old self with its practices and have put on the new self, which is being renewed in knowledge in the image of its Creator' (Colossians 3:9).

Out of darkness into light

Peter and Paul also like the picture of light coming where there was once darkness. The Bible often links light and life (see Psalms 36:9; 56:13). As we stated in the last chapter, this idea is in the background in John 3.

Charles Wesley captured the picture well when he wrote these famous lines:

Long my imprisoned spirit lay
Fast bound in sin and nature's night.
Thine eye diffused a quickening ray,
I woke the dungeon flamed with light.
My chains fell off, my heart was free,
I rose, went forth and followed Thee.

Peter speaks of Christians singing 'the praises of him who called you out of darkness into his wonderful light' (1 Peter 2:9). Paul says to believers, 'For you were once darkness, but now you are light in the Lord. Live as children of light (for the fruit of the light consists in all goodness, righteousness and truth)' (Ephesians 5:8-9). We have come into the kingdom of light for God 'has rescued us from the dominion of darkness and brought us into the kingdom of the Son he loves' (Colossians 1:13), so 'you, brothers, are not in darkness … You are all sons of the light and sons of the day. We do not belong to the night or to the darkness' (1 Thessalonians 5:4-5). It is when he opens our eyes that we see wonderful things in his law (Psalm 119:18). What a blessing to have seeing eyes and hearing ears (Matthew 13:16).

At the end of 1747, Jonathan Edwards preached a series of sermons on Acts 26:18 where Paul is told that God is going to send him to the Gentiles,

to open their eyes and turn them from darkness to light, and from the power of Satan to God, so that they may receive forgiveness of sins and a place among those who are sanctified by faith in me.

Edwards remarks how 'in saving conversion they that are blind and in darkness have their eyes opened and are turned from darkness unto light'. The picture of blindness and sight is used in different ways in Scripture but it well illustrates the new birth.

Yet another picture is in the background here, as seen in Colossians 1:13. It is that of passing from one world to another, out of Satan's realm into God's kingdom. It is similar to Jesus' idea of taking a different path. In John 8:12 he says, 'Whoever follows me will never walk in darkness, but will have the light of life.' These words have their roots in Proverbs 4:18: 'The path of the righteous is like the first gleam of dawn, shining ever brighter till the full light of day.'

In Ephesians 4:18 Paul says of unbelievers, 'They are darkened in their understanding and separated from the life of God because of the ignorance that is in them due to the hardening of their hearts.' He uses three related images to convey the unbeliever's plight. They are darkened in their understanding, separated from the life of God and ignorant due to the hardening of their hearts. The only remedy is for the light to shine, life to begin and the hard heart to be softened or replaced. This is what happens when a person is born again and they find Jesus to be the light, the way, the truth and the life.

Baptism with the Holy Spirit

In his excellent little book on *The New Birth* Professor Andy McGowan says that 'Baptism with the Holy Spirit refers to new birth.' Before Jesus' ministry commenced, John the Baptist prophesied (Matthew 3:11, etc.) that his successor would 'baptize you with the Holy Spirit'. After Jesus' resurrection his disciples are told that 'John baptized with water, but in a few days you will be baptized with the Holy Spirit' (Acts 1:5; cf. 11:16). The Spirit is then poured out on the Day of Pentecost and throughout Acts we read of various people receiving the Spirit as they accept the gospel message. Clearly the 'mini-pentecosts' in Acts 8, 10 and 19 have unusual aspects to them but they involve the regeneration of sinners by the Spirit.

> The only remedy is for the light to shine, life to begin and the hard heart to be softened or replaced.

Some have suggested that baptism in or by the Spirit is something that follows conversion but, in fact, it should be identified with the new birth. In 1 Corinthians 12:13 Paul says to the believers that they were *all* 'baptized by one Spirit into one body — whether Jews or Greeks, slave or free — and we were all given the one Spirit to drink'. This baptism in the Spirit is the same as the baptism into Christ spoken of in Romans 6. In Romans 6:4 Paul ties it to the resurrection language we have already noted above.

> We were therefore buried with him through baptism into death in order that, just as Christ was raised from the dead through the glory of the Father, we too may live a new life.

73

If we identify baptism in the Spirit and sealing, Ephesians 1:13 could be a problem. It says there, *'having believed*, you were marked in him with a seal, the promised Holy Spirit'. A seal is a mark of ownership. This could suggest that believing precedes that mark of ownership. As with the resurrection picture mentioned above, we need to take care how we express ourselves. Perhaps it would be better to say that the baptism of the Spirit immediately produces faith and that faith leads straight to the sealing spoken of here. It is as we believe that it becomes evident that the Spirit is in us, proving that we belong to the Father.

Variety

It is clear that the Bible uses a variety of pictures to convey the idea that the Christian life starts with a radical change produced by God. In the last chapter, we mentioned the ideas of washing, receiving a new heart or spirit, God's law in the mind and on the heart, and circumcision of the heart, found initially in the Old Testament. Here we have spoken of a new birth, a new planting, a new creation, a resurrection, a passing from darkness to light, entering a new world, setting out in a new direction, Spirit baptism and being irresistibly drawn. God intends all these pictures to add to our understanding of regeneration and we do well to reflect on them. Is your understanding of new birth all that it should be?

6.
Why is it necessary?

'In reply Jesus declared, "I tell you the truth, no one can see the kingdom of God unless he is born again"'
(John 3:3).

Next we consider various facets of the question of why new birth is necessary, namely biblical teaching on new birth, sin, God's character, how to please him and the nature of heaven.

In the eighteenth century George Whitefield preached hundreds of times (perhaps even more than a thousand times), on the text 'You must be born again.' Someone once asked him why he preached that particular message so often. His answer was simple but profound: 'Because you *must* be born again.'

The mystic Scheffler put it quaintly:

Had Christ a thousand times,
Been born in Bethlehem,
But not in thee, thy sin
Would still thy soul condemn.

When I was in school, I did not get on very well with mathematics. One of my problems was that it seemed so irrelevant. Why do we need to know about it? What use is it? In exploring the subject of regeneration we have seen something of what it is and what it is not. At this point, it will be useful to take a step back and ask *why* the new birth is so vital. Why *must* we all be born again?

Calvin says very simply that 'Man must be born again, because he is flesh.' Our very creatureliness makes new birth necessary. 'The grace of God', he says, 'has no charms for men till the Holy Spirit gives them a taste for it.'

Thomas Goodwin stresses the fact that without new birth the work of the Father in seeking to glorify his holiness and grace, and of the Son in seeking reconciliation between God and man, is incomplete and therefore useless. He also sees the chief reason for new birth as being that God's image will be reproduced in us. As a result we will conform to him in readiness to do what pleases him and will view his glory as our great goal.

The whole Bible teaches us that a man must be born again to enter God's kingdom, or even to see it, but we can best approach the question on the following lines. Regeneration is necessary because of what the Bible says about five things — regeneration itself, the sinfulness of sin, God's character, pleasing God and the nature of heaven.

Regeneration itself

If we simply confine ourselves, firstly, to what the Bible says about the new birth itself, we immediately see that being reborn is not an optional extra for Christian living. It is not a de luxe add-on, a bonus, an extra, something reserved only for 'first-class travel'. Rather it is something vital. It is indispensable. It is not an elegant window giving us a view of the glory of God's house but the very door into it. Without this there can be no entrance. It is not a mere sniff at the delicacies in God's kingdom but a real taste of what he has to offer, a feast that will enter our bodies and do eternal good. Without it we will starve. If you are not born again, you are simply not a Christian at all.

> [Being born again] is not an elegant window giving us a view of the glory of God's house but the very door into it.

Speaking to Nicodemus in John 3, Jesus makes clear more than once that new birth is essential. In John 3:3 he says plainly, 'I tell you the truth, no one can see the kingdom of God unless he is born again.' In 3:5-6 he is emphatic:

I tell you the truth, no one can enter the kingdom of God unless he is born of water and the Spirit. Flesh gives birth to flesh, but the Spirit gives birth to spirit.

In 3:7 he sums up briefly but unmistakably: 'You must be born again.'

Matthew 18:3 is similar in some ways, 'I tell you the truth, unless you change and become like little children, you will never enter the kingdom of heaven.' The new birth is imperative. 'No one can come to me unless the Father who sent me draws him' (John 6:44). Natural descent, human decision and a husband's will are unavailing. What matters is being born of God (John 1:12-13).

Paul is equally clear. Galatians 6:15: 'Neither circumcision nor uncircumcision means anything; what counts is a new creation.' This is the new creation he speaks of in 2 Corinthians 5:17 and which characterizes all who are in Christ. He had earlier declared 'that flesh and blood cannot inherit the kingdom of God, nor does the perishable inherit the imperishable' (1 Corinthians 15:50).

The sinfulness of sin

Archibald Alexander wrote that 'The proof of the wickedness of man is found in every part of the Bible.' He also said that depravity 'is a truth confirmed by all history and experience'. We begin with the Bible and these verses:

- 'Who can say, "I have kept my heart pure; I am clean and without sin?"' (Proverbs 20:9).
- 'There is not a righteous man on earth who does what is right and never sins' (Ecclesiastes 7:20).

The truth about man is that every inclination of the thoughts of his heart is only evil all the time, even from childhood. With

David I have to say I was 'sinful at birth, sinful from the time my mother conceived me' (Genesis 6:5; 8:21; Psalm 51:5).

We have looked at some of the pictures the Bible uses to speak of regeneration. These often begin with a very bleak description of the unregenerate. When Paul speaks of Christians being made 'alive with Christ' (Ephesians 2:5) he refers firstly to how they were by nature dead in transgressions and sins (2:1). Does not the very idea of being born again imply that the person who has not known it is lifeless and a spiritual non-entity?

We are not saying we are all as bad as one another, or that people do not do relatively good things. It is better to help an old lady across a road than rob her. It is better to give to a good cause than squander money. It is better to be a faithful spouse than sleep around. When we remember, however, that 'The LORD does not look at the things man looks at. Man looks at the outward appearance, but the LORD looks at the heart' (1 Samuel 16:7), we begin to see that no one has even begun to reach his standards.

Sometimes Christians describe becoming a Christian using the figure of a beggar finding bread. This is fine as far as it goes, but the biblical picture is closer to that of a dead man being brought to life. The change needed is less like a veterinary surgeon sewing up a wound in the paw of some poor creature and more like the total transformation involved when a caterpillar becomes a butterfly.

We have to say, in William Tidd Mason's words, not only 'Lord, I was blind, deaf and dumb' but also,

Lord I was dead! I could not stir
My lifeless soul to come to Thee.

We need to be quickened to 'rise from sin's dark sepulchre'. If we say, to use another common picture, man's plight is like that of a drowning man yelling out to be saved, we have again not gone far enough. Edwin Palmer is surely more biblical when he says the true picture is:

> ...a man at the bottom of the ocean in the Marianas Trench more than 35,000 feet deep. The weight of the water on top of him is six tons for every square inch. He has been there for 1,000 years and the sharks have eaten his heart.

Elsewhere he says that man's intellect, will and emotions all need to change.

- *His intellect is fallen.* Man cannot understand God. He is blind and needs the veil to be taken from his unbelieving heart. It is removed only in Christ (2 Corinthians 3:12-16).
- *His will is fallen.* He cannot serve God. A slave to sin, he is unwilling and unable to serve God (John 8:34; Romans 8:7). Only by the Spirit can he vanquish sin (Romans 8:13).
- *His emotions are fallen.* He cannot love God. 'The sinful mind is hostile to God' (Romans 8:7). Reconciliation is possible only in Christ.

Another verse that stresses man's predicament is Romans 7:18. Paul says things are so bad 'that nothing good lives in me, that is, in my sinful nature'. He has already spoken of man in most unpromising terms in the early chapters. Romans 1:18 speaks of 'all the godlessness and wickedness of men who suppress the truth by their wickedness'. It refers to man's futile thinking and the darkness of his foolish heart. Chapter 2 speaks of the emptiness of mere outward religion. In 3:10-18, Paul marshals a catena (chain) of Old Testament verses beginning:

There is no one righteous, not even one; there is no one who understands, no one who seeks God. All have turned away, they have together become worthless; there is no one who does good, not even one.

Romans 8:6-8 contrasts believer and unbeliever in the strongest terms. We read:

The mind of sinful man is death, but the mind controlled by the Spirit is life and peace; the sinful mind is hostile to God. It does not submit to God's law, nor can it do so. Those controlled by the sinful nature cannot please God.

Could the prospect of coming to Christ be put in less promising terms? No wonder Paul says that 'The man without the Spirit does not accept the things that come from the Spirit of God' (1 Corinthians 2:14). The problem is that they 'are foolishness to him'. In fact, 'he cannot understand them'. This, of course, is because they are spiritually discerned. Without the Spirit's regenerating work they can never be grasped.

Preachers often quote Jeremiah's question (Jeremiah 13:23) in this context: 'Can the Ethiopian change his skin or the leopard its spots? Neither can you do good who are accustomed to doing evil.' It is our nature to do evil. We have no more

> It is our nature to do evil. We have no more prospect of changing that nature by ourselves than a man with black skin has of turning it white.

prospect of changing that nature by ourselves than a man with black skin has of turning it white or a leopard has of exchanging its spots for tiger stripes. What about Ezekiel's vision of the valley of dry bones? Only a powerful movement of God's Spirit transformed that situation. Nothing else could have had any impact.

Then there is Jesus's reference to entering the kingdom being as difficult as for a camel to go through the eye of a needle (Mark 10:25). We have also noted Luke 15:24, 32, where the father in the parable says his son was not just lost but *dead* before being found and made alive again.

As for the confirmation 'in all history and experience' American pastor Russell Smith sums up:

Literature, history, political philosophy all point us back to this truth — depravity. I don't like thinking about depravity. I like to think I'm a pretty decent, likeable guy. I like to think that everyone is basically reasonable and if just left alone we'd all get along just fine. But then I keep rubbing up against the truths in literature, history and philosophy. I keep reading the newspaper and seeing evidence of depravity all about. Worse for me is when I look into my own heart ... I have to face the disturbing truth that depravity is real — honest self-examination proves it so.

As J. C. Ryle says, 'The man who denies the universal necessity of regeneration can know very little of the heart's corruption.' Pardon is not enough. 'The image of God, which sin has blotted out, must be restored.' Something very powerful indeed is needed to bring about such a change.

Reformed teacher Herman Hoeksema says that because man loves the darkness rather than the light,

> he certainly will not make any attempt to come to the light. He will rather avoid it, despise and hate the light … For the natural man there is no hope of improvement or reformation in the way of education or in the way of a better example or in the way of exercising himself in the discipline of external virtue. In that way he will never enter into the kingdom of God.

An old hymn says starkly but rightly:

> Our nature's totally deprav'd
> The heart a sink of sin;
> Without a change we can't be saved;
> We must be born again.

The character of God

The other side of this coin is the truth that God is 'too pure to look on evil', 'cannot tolerate wrong' and is one in whose eyes 'even the heavens are not pure' (Habakkuk 1:13; Job 15:15). He is a God who is holy (Leviticus 11:44; 19:2), 'righteous in all his ways' (Psalm 145:17). The Ten Commandments make clear the sort of people he wants us to be but we have all 'sinned and fall short of the glory of God'; 'We all, like sheep, have gone astray, each of us has turned to his own way' (Romans 3:23; Isaiah 53:6).

'Do two walk together unless they have agreed to do so?' (Amos 3:3). Or, as 2 Corinthians 6:14-16 states:

> For what do righteousness and wickedness have in common? or what fellowship can light have with darkness? What harmony is there between Christ and Belial?

John Murray has written of regeneration and of Christ:

> It is the logical link between his teaching respecting man's depravity, on the one hand, and his teaching respecting the demands and requirements of the kingdom of God on the other. The Sermon on the Mount would be unintelligible without the presupposition of the new birth.

The Bible speaks of God's wrath against sin in many places. Asaph says,

> In the hand of the LORD is a cup full of foaming wine mixed with spices; he pours it out, and all the wicked of the earth drink it down to its very dregs
>
> (Psalm 75:8).

Nahum declares (Nahum 1:2):

The LORD is a jealous and avenging God; the LORD takes vengeance and is filled with wrath. The LORD takes vengeance on his foes and maintains his wrath against his enemies.

Paul speaks of how God's wrath is already being revealed (Romans 1:18) and warns that to remain stubborn and unrepentant in heart is to store up 'wrath against yourself for the day of God's wrath, when his righteous judgement will be revealed' (Romans 2:5). When he warns the Ephesians against 'sexual immorality … impurity … greed … obscenity, foolish talk or coarse joking' (vv.3-4), he then says, 'Let no one deceive you with empty words, for because of such things God's wrath comes on those who are disobedient' (Ephesians 5:6). Revelation 16:19 speaks of 'the cup filled with the wine of the fury of his wrath'.

Reflecting on the Bible's teaching, former theological principal Eryl Davies has defined God's wrath as 'the controlled and permanent opposition of God's holy nature to all sin'. Given its existence, it is certain then that without some great change, no one will ever be acceptable to God. It is only when we see ourselves, in Jonathan Edwards' famous words, as 'sinners in the hands of an angry God' that we realize our desperate need of rebirth.

It is in the wake of the second birth that communion with God becomes possible and we know fellowship 'with the Father and with his Son, Jesus Christ' (1 John 1:3).

Pleasing God

It is true that unbelievers can do what is relatively good but without new birth they cannot do what is truly good and pleasing to God. Without regeneration, a man has no true faith and so can never satisfy God. Hebrews 11:6 reminds us that 'without faith it is impossible to please God'. It is those who are born of God who receive Jesus by faith and who believe he is the Christ (John 1:12-13; 1 John 5:1). Faith is a flower that will only grow where the field has been prepared and transformed.

'To those who are corrupted and do not believe, nothing is pure. In fact, both their minds and consciences are corrupted.' They may claim to know God but their actions deny him. 'They are detestable, disobedient and unfit for doing anything good' (Titus 1:15-16).

Being a new creation is what counts (Galatians 6:15) and to suppose that any action on our part, without new birth, is going to please God is plain wrong. In fact, such a person, in Boston's words, has shut the door with the thief still in the house. Although we will have more to say about this later, it is true that his prayers are an abomination to God (Proverbs 15:8). Inevitably, selfishness and an unchanged heart will dog his every step.

Praying and seeking God are good for all, reborn or not, but to play the hypocrite and pretend to others or to ourselves that we have been changed within when nothing of the sort has happened is a great evil. By nature, we cannot be pleasing to God.

The nature of heaven

Another way to approach the question is to consider what is necessary to make a man fit for heaven and to gain him admittance to that holy place.

By this stage in history, we are familiar with the fact that it is impossible for a man to survive in outer space without artificial support. It is one of the great barriers to any idea of colonizing the moon. The moon's atmosphere is alien to human life. Man is no more able to live unaided on the moon than he is to fly like a bird in the air or live like a fish in the sea.

It is equally true that man is not suited to life in heaven. The problem is not a lack of oxygen, a surfeit of water or an inability to fly. Rather the problem is moral. In heaven all things centre on God and, by nature, this is not man's inclination.

Alexander puts it this way:

Heaven is a holy place, and all the exercises and employments are holy, therefore, 'Without holiness no man shall see the Lord.' And to be holy, ye must be born again.

A. W. Pink declares that new birth is 'indispensably necessary before any soul can enter heaven. In order to love spiritual things a man must be made spiritual.' He goes on:

> None can dwell with God and be eternally happy in His presence until a radical change has been wrought in him, a change from sin to holiness; and this change must take place on earth.

As he says, an unregenerate person may hear about the way to heaven, he may correctly understand biblical teaching but he cannot love these things and rejoice in them as the believer does: 'They perish because they refused to love the truth and so be saved' (2 Thessalonians 2:10).

> How could one possibly enter a world of ineffable holiness who has spent all of his time in sin, i.e. pleasing self? How could he possibly sing the song of the Lamb if his heart had never been tuned unto it? How could he endure to behold the awful majesty of God face to face who never before so much as saw Him 'through a glass darkly' by the eye of faith? As it is excruciating torture for eyes that have long been confined to dismal darkness to suddenly gaze upon the bright beams of the midday sun, so will it be when the unregenerate behold Him who is light.

God is 'not a God who takes pleasure in evil; with you the wicked cannot dwell'. The pure in heart are the ones who get to see him (Psalm 5:4; Hebrews 12:14; Matthew 5:8). The highway to heaven is 'the Way of Holiness. The unclean will not journey on it; it will be for those who walk in that Way; wicked fools will not go about on it' (Isaiah 35:8). Anyone who lives in the ways Paul mentions in Galatians 5:19-21 (immorality, idolatry, drunkenness, etc.) 'will not inherit the kingdom of God'.

When the New Jerusalem comes down out of heaven, it will truly be the holy city and, as Isaiah says, 'The uncircumcised and defiled will not enter you again' (52:1). 'Nothing impure will ever enter it, nor will anyone who does what is shameful or deceitful, but only those whose names are written in the Lamb's book of life' (Revelation 21:27). Jesus is going to send out his angels and the Son of Man will 'weed out of his kingdom everything that causes sin and all who do evil' (Matthew 13:41).

This means, as Ryle has observed, that we can reach heaven without many things but not without being born again. Hoekema agrees. By nature, we have no place in God's kingdom nor 'even a remote conception of the things of that kingdom'. We have no desire for such things. We delight in and live in another kingdom, that of the Prince of Darkness. God's kingdom is quite different. It is 'spiritual, ethical and heavenly in essence and nature. It is not of the world, but it is of the Father. It is not from below, but it is from above.' This is why no one who is born only 'according to the flesh' can see it. As Phil Ryken puts it: 'It takes a new birth to see the new world.'

You have to be qualified to 'share in the inheritance of the saints in the kingdom of light' (Colossians 1:12). As Boston points out, the unregenerate have no place in heaven. It is not their native country (see Hebrews 11:16; Philippians 3:19) and there is nothing there they will enjoy. It is a holy place and they have no desire for holiness. They would not appreciate the company, the employment there (praising God) or the fact that it went on for ever.

The hearts of stone such people have will sink them into hell. Their lack of fruit means the axe will soon be employed to bring them down.

It is clear then that regeneration is absolutely necessary. What the Bible says about the new birth, sin, God's character and how to please him, and the nature of heaven shows this. Regeneration is no luxury, no supplement. If you are not born again you cannot be a Christian. You are still in your sins. God has shut the door to heaven fast against you. You must be born again.

With Charles Wesley we must say,

I must be born again, or die
To all eternity.

7.
What brings it about?

'Praise be to the God and Father of our Lord Jesus Christ! In his great mercy he has given us new birth into a living hope through the resurrection of Jesus Christ from the dead ... you have been born again, not of perishable seed, but of imperishable, through the living and enduring word of God'
(1 Peter 1:3, 23).

We now consider what causes new birth. We will do so from various angles, considering its fundamental, qualifying and instrumental causes.

We have seen something of what regeneration is and why it is necessary. We come now to the question of what it is that causes a person to be born again. There is really more than one answer to this question; it all depends on what is meant by the word *causes*. We will consider, then, the fundamental cause of regeneration, the basis on which new birth takes place and the means by which people most often come to it.

The fundamental cause — not man but God

We think first of the origin of regeneration. Second birth is not something we bring about for ourselves, any more than we bring about our first birth. 'That man cannot regenerate himself is too evident to need a remark,' wrote Archibald Alexander. We cannot bring it about for anyone else either. A spiritual resurrection is just as impossible for us as any sort of physical resurrection would be. It is something God does.

The origin of the whole operation lies in God. This is clear from a verse such as John 3:16, which clearly places the origin of salvation in him.

> For God so loved the world that he gave his one and only Son, that whoever believes in him shall not perish but have eternal life.

He is the one who *chooses* to give new birth (James 1:18). Ephesians 2:4-5 reminds believers how:

> because of his great love for us, God, who is rich in mercy, made us alive with Christ even when we were dead in transgressions — it is by grace you have been saved.

George Swinnock asks why some are hardened like clay and some melt like wax, why some receive light from the fiery pillar and some are in the dark, why some cross the Red Sea and others drown in it. Why is the truth hidden from the wise and learned but revealed to little children? Jesus is clear, 'Yes,

What brings it about?

Father, for this was your good pleasure' (Matthew 11:26). We need to grasp this so that, like Charles Wesley, we will realize that God's power and God's alone,

> Can change the leper's spots
> And melt the heart of stone.

We have drawn attention previously to Deuteronomy 30:6 and Ezekiel 36:26-27 as Old Testament verses that speak of regeneration. Notice that in the first it is, 'The LORD your God' who 'will circumcise your hearts and the hearts of your descendants'. In the second, it is again God who is active.

> *I* will give you a new heart and put a new spirit in you; *I* will remove from you your heart of stone and give you a heart of flesh. And *I* will put *my Spirit* in you and move you to follow my decrees and be careful to keep my laws [italics mine].

As for New Testament Scriptures, new birth is brought about not by 'natural descent … human decision or a husband's will', but by God. Men plant and water, but God makes things grow. He saves, but not because of righteous things we have done. It is because of his mercy that he washes in rebirth and renews by the Spirit. In his great mercy, *he* gives new birth into a living hope through the resurrection of Jesus Christ from the dead. Doing right is possible only because we have been born of *him* (see John 1:13; 1 Corinthians 3:6; Titus 3:5; 1 Peter 1:3; 1 John 2:29).

It is right then for Christians to sing together:

Hallelujah! Let praises ring!
Unto the Holy Ghost we sing
For our regeneration.
The saving faith in us *He* wrought
And us unto the Bridegroom brought,
Made us his chosen nation.

It is the Holy Spirit in particular who brings the change about. 'No one can say, "Jesus is Lord," except by the Holy Spirit' (1 Corinthians 12:3). He is the great writer, the great artist, the cleanser and renewer of hearts. It is *the Spirit of the living God* who writes *not on tablets of stone but on tablets of human hearts* to reveal believers as *a letter from Christ*. The transforming art of changing people into Christ's *likeness with ever-increasing glory* so that they reflect his glory *comes from the Lord, who is the Spirit*. He is the one who brings about the new birth itself (2 Corinthians 3:8, 18; Titus 3:5-6).

> [The Holy Spirit] is the great writer, the great artist, the cleanser and renewer of hearts.

The qualifying cause — Christ and his atoning death

In 1974 Lenny Smith wrote the popular hymn 'Our God reigns'. It includes the lines:

His life ran down upon the ground like pouring rain
That we might be born again.

What brings it about?

We can speak, secondly, of what qualifies a person to be reborn. Peter links new birth to the resurrection (1 Peter 1:3) but if we ask on what basis new birth can fairly take place, we say it is because of the blood of Christ or his atoning death. It is his propitiatory sacrifice that secures regeneration. As John Murray put it — he has *accomplished* redemption, which is then *applied* in regeneration and the other aspects of salvation.

By the Fall, man was rendered guilty, ruined and helpless. It would have been perfectly just for God to have left us in that state and done nothing for us, as was the case with the angels that fell. He owes us nothing. But God created man for his own glory and was unwilling that all should be left to perish.

In his wisdom and goodness, and according to his great mercy, he did all that was necessary for his people to be saved, including providing atonement for each one through Jesus Christ.

On the atonement we can say several things. First, that it was prefigured in the Old Testament period. Under Moses various sacrifices were instituted with the temple worship and the Levitical priesthood to teach men what was needed and to provide a pattern for the future. The sacrifices were made on the behalf of others, involving penal substitutionary atonement. Leviticus 4, for example, speaks of the sacrificer laying 'his hand on the head of the sin offering' (v. 28) before slaughtering it, and describes the priest sacrificing the animal as 'making atonement for the man's sin' (v. 31), so that he is forgiven. Many parallels are drawn between the temple worship and Jesus' atoning death, especially in the book of Hebrews.

Some New Testament passages speak directly of Christ being a *propitiation* for sin (Romans 3:25; 1 John 2:2; 4:10). This word refers to an offering designed to turn away wrath. On the cross, Jesus Christ turned away the Father's wrath by the atoning sacrifice of himself. The New Testament also speaks of the cross as an act of reconciliation (2 Corinthians 5:18-20; Romans 5:10; Colossians 1:20; Hebrews 2:17). By nature there is enmity between man and God but through the cross there can be peace.

Further, Christ is also spoken of as a ransom for sin. A ransom is paid to secure a person's release. He 'gave himself as a ransom' (1 Timothy 2:6). He himself said that he 'did not come to be served, but to serve, and to give his life as a ransom for many' (Mark 10:45). By his precious blood he paid the price to release many from their sins. He is the Redeemer and Saviour of his people.

There are many references to 'the redemption that came by Christ Jesus' (Matthew 1:21; 18:11, etc.). Other relevant passages include Isaiah 53:4-8; Mark 8:37; Romans 3:24; Romans 4:25; 5:6-10, etc.

More broadly, Jesus was:

Born to raise the sons of earth,
Born to give them second birth.

His birth led to his atoning death and resurrection. We think of the atonement most readily in connection with justification and link the resurrection with the new birth. The atonement was necessary, however, for both. Without it, there would be no basis for regeneration. Because of all that Christ has done, God is willing to grant rebirth to his own that they may receive the full benefit of Christ's redemption.

In Isaac Watts' words:

'Tis through the purchase of his death
Who hung upon the tree,
The Spirit is sent down to breathe
On such dry bones as we.

One other thing perhaps worth mentioning here is that the notion that regeneration is rooted in what happened *between* Christ's death and resurrection is an unhelpful teaching with no basis in Scripture. The idea takes the phrase 'he descended into hell' in what is usually called *The Apostles' Creed* to mean that after he died Jesus went to hell in his spirit. When he was raised again, some assert, he became the first born-again man.

We are wiser to take the phrase about descending into hell to refer to what Jesus suffered on the cross. Remember that Jesus told the dying thief that he would be with him in paradise that very day. The idea of Jesus descending to hell for three days at his death, though quite an ancient idea, is thoroughly unsound. No, the new birth is possible on the basis of what Christ did on the cross and when he rose from the dead, confirming that his atoning death was acceptable to God.

Instrumental cause — God's Word

It is quite natural to say that when Lazarus was raised from the dead, it was through the voice of Jesus speaking to him. If we are more precise, of course, we have to admit that Lazarus came to life before that moment or he could not have heard Jesus calling him out. To pray with Wesley, then,

Strike with the hammer of Thy Word,
And break these hearts of stone,

is quite legitimate, provided we remember that words in and of themselves can do nothing.

Regarding his parable of the sower, Jesus says, 'The seed is the word of God' (Luke 8:11). It is when the seed falls into the good soil that it takes root and produces a crop. Paul speaks of preaching to the Corinthians as sowing 'spiritual seed' among them (1 Corinthians 9:11). The suggestion is not that words themselves have the germ of life in them but that it is through the God-applied word that people are converted.

There are verses in the New Testament that speak of regeneration in a broader sense than is usual when they refer to God using the means of his word to reveal signs of life. Thus James reminds his readers that God 'chose to give us birth through the word of truth, that we might be a kind of firstfruits of all he created' (1:18). Similarly Peter says, 'For you have been born again, not of perishable seed, but of imperishable, through the living and enduring word of God' (1 Peter 1:23). Ephesians 5:26 refers to 'the washing with water through the word' and is another appropriate reference here.

All three speak of renewal *through* God's word. They speak of the word as 'the word of truth' and 'the living and enduring word of God'.

It is effective in fostering God-given life, firstly, because it is *true*. Remember Jesus' words where he prays to the Father to 'sanctify' his disciples 'by the truth' (John 17:17). He then says 'your word is truth'. It is by this means then that the Son sets men free (John 8:36).

Secondly, the word is *living and enduring*. Hebrews 4:12 says of this 'living and active' word of God that it is 'sharper than any double-edged sword' and can penetrate 'even to dividing soul and spirit, joints and marrow; it judges the thoughts and attitudes of the heart.' Such a word can deal with men's souls and renew them.

Finally, it is *God's* Word and so is well able to bring about his purposes: 'The law of the LORD is perfect, reviving [or converting] the soul' (Psalm 19:7).

The word is the means of second birth, to quote an old writer, 'because God has connected the influences of the Spirit with the preaching and reading of the Word'. It is through the 'foolishness' of what Christians preach that God saves people. The word stirs us to think and to feel in a spiritual way: 'The Spirit operates by and through the word.' The 'power and penetrating energy' that the word has comes from the Spirit: 'Without the omnipotence of God the word would be as inefficient as clay and spittle, to restore sight to the blind.'

> It is through the 'foolishness' of what Christians preach that God saves people.

So 'while Peter was still speaking' the words he spoke to Cornelius and others, 'the Holy Spirit came on all who heard the message' (Acts 10:44).

In Luke's description of Lydia's conversion you see the order quite clearly (Acts 16:14). First, she listens to Paul preach, then the Lord opens her heart, then she responds to Paul's message.

It is because of this instrumental element that Paul can say to the Corinthians, 'in Christ Jesus I became your father through the gospel' (1 Corinthians 4:15). This is the reason too why preaching is so important if people are to be born again. As Paul asks (Romans 10:14):

> How, then, can they call on the one they have not believed in? And how can they believe in the one of whom they have not heard? And how can they hear without someone preaching to them?

Throughout the New Testament we see this pattern of preachers being sent out with the Word that people may be born again. Like John the Baptist, Christ himself came preaching the Word and so did his apostles after him. He sent them out saying, 'Go into all the world and preach the good news to all creation' (Mark 16:15). It is as we preach God's Word that people are born again. We know that God is able to work when, where and how he chooses to work, but it is noticeable that where men go out and preach in his name people are born again; but where they are not able to do that, such things are much more scarce.

Like Ezekiel, we are to preach to the dry bones and trust the Spirit of God to bring life. People need to accept 'the word planted in you, which can save you' not merely listening to the word but doing what it says (James 1:21-22). Paul tells how he came to Thessalonica and preached successfully. What made the difference was that they accepted his preaching 'not as the word of men, but as it actually is, the word of God, which is at work in you who believe'. This is why they turned 'to God from idols to serve the living and true God' (1 Thessalonians 2:13; 1 Thessalonians 1:9).

When we ask what causes the new birth, therefore, we must say that it originates with God who transforms people by the Spirit, and it is possible because of what Christ has done on the cross. It usually happens as the Word of God is preached.

In the face of this biblical understanding we must not suppose that there is nothing to be done but to wait for God to work. The Bible does not encourage us to think like that. Philippians 2:12-13 says, 'Continue to work out your salvation with fear and trembling.' Why? 'For it is God who works in you to will and to act according to his good purpose.' God's work in man should be the stimulus to our working.

John Angell James' *Anxious Enquirer* compares our part to that of sailors hoisting their sails to catch the breeze that God sends to waft the ship along, or to farmers ploughing or sowing, reliant on the sunshine and rain that God sends for germination and growth.

He says of the man with the withered hand in Matthew 12 that when the Lord commanded him to stretch out his hand, 'he did not say, Lord, I cannot, it is dead'. Rather, he relied on the power of the one who told him what to do, 'believing that the command implied a promise of help, if he were willing to receive it'. He willed to stretch it out and was able.

The command then is 'Repent and believe.' Do not say, 'I can't because I'm dead in sin.' Rather, believe in the promise of grace to help and obey, depending on him who works in men to will and to act according to his good purpose.

We will return to this theme in our final chapter.

8.
When does it happen?

'Then he said, "Jesus, remember me when you come into your kingdom." Jesus answered him, "I tell you the truth, today you will be with me in paradise"'
(Luke 23:42-43).

We will now consider the diversity of experience that those who are born again may know in light of their age, vigour, knowledge and temperament, and include examples.

I remember as a boy being told by my mother that the Queen of England was very special because she has two birthdays — an actual one and an official one. As a child, the idea of two birthdays sounded very attractive.

If you are a Christian, you also, in a manner of speaking, have two birthdays. When the Kent martyr Alice Potkins was arrested in 1556, she was asked her age. She replied that she was forty-nine 'according to her old age' but only one 'according to her young age, since she learned Christ'. Many could say something similar. Take myself as an example. I was first born on 22 May 1959. I know the date because my parents brought me up to mark the day and I have a piece of paper somewhere with the details on it. Some twelve years later, I was born again, probably on 16 April 1972. I am a little more hazy on this in some ways but I remember the period and I have another piece of paper somewhere marking the date.

On occasions, I have met people who cannot tell you accurately when they were born. I remember a Vietnamese fellow who was picked up on the streets of Saigon (Ho Chi Minh City) as an orphaned toddler, and was eventually brought up in the UK. He only knew more or less how old he was. Many abandoned children share the same sort of ignorance. In certain parts of rural Nigeria, it is common not to know the exact day you were born as records are not kept too strictly. In a similar way, many Christians do not know exactly when they were born again. As Archibald Alexander points out, even those who claim that they do know may well be wrong.

I have just given you the date 16 April 1972, but I recognize that I may be mistaken on this. All I really know is that on that date I made a firm dedication of myself to God and that I have subsequent reason to believe that I have been reborn. As for the exact date, I may have it wrong.

Westminster Theological Seminary founder J. Gresham Machen once described an experience-meeting he had attended where people were asked to share where they were born the first time, and when and where they were born the second time. Many were glad to do this but one woman, having answered the first question, stated that although she was definitely converted she could not say when and where.

103

Machen commented:

> I do believe that there is a definite instant when the wonderful event occurs in the life of everyone who becomes a Christian — the wonderful event when he or she is born again — but I do believe also that there are many who cannot tell when that instant was; it is known to God, but not to them.

He goes on to say that we must not think the one experience inferior to the other. Spurgeon makes the same point in his usual pithy way:

> If you are really born of God, the date of your new birth is interesting to curiosity but not important to piety.

> A characteristic of regeneration is that it is mysterious and secret so ... it can be difficult to know exactly when it has occurred.

A characteristic of regeneration is that it is mysterious and secret so we should not be surprised that it can be difficult to know exactly when it has occurred. We have shown that it is vital, however, and so it is good to consider now the fact that although the second birth is essential for all, the actual experience of discovering you are born again can show some variety.

Part of this arises, of course, from how far one has gone in sin. Although we must be careful how we state it, there is surely a difference, at least outwardly, between someone who has grown up in a Christian home and has never outwardly rebelled against the faith and someone who has gone some distance in sin. This is bound to affect the way that the new birth is experienced.

In the opening chapters of his fascinating book, *Thoughts on religious experience*, Professor Alexander identifies four factors that affect the course of conversion. None of these things can affect regeneration itself, of course. As we have emphasized, that is something that God himself does. However, the way we perceive regeneration in ourselves and in others can be affected by any or all of these factors.

The age factor

One obvious factor is the way in which different people are born again at different ages. In Scripture we know that Timothy came to faith at a relatively young age, while someone like the Philippian gaoler was probably an older man when he was regenerated. Their experiences were quite different, perhaps because of these, as well as other factors.

Although many people are converted in their late teens or early twenties, many are converted at other ages and there is every reason to suppose that people can be, and are in fact, born again at every age between nought and ninety, and even perhaps outside those boundaries in some rare instances.

A. A. Hodge's *Outlines of theology* raises the question of whether 'infants are susceptible of regeneration; and, if so, what is the nature of regeneration in them?' Infants and adults alike, he says, are rational and moral beings, affected by total depravity. The difference is that with adults their faculties are more developed. Given all that we have said about regeneration, there is no reason why babies, in the womb or out of it, may not be born again as easily as adults. 'In both cases,' says Hodge, 'the operation is miraculous, and therefore inscrutable.'

As for Scripture support for this, Hodge turns, like others, to the case of John the Baptist. This makes sense but his references to Luke 18:15-16 and Acts 2:39 are more dubious. Alexander mentions Jeremiah 1:5, which again does not say exactly what he suggests. The story of Samuel is perhaps more relevant.

These men are not suggesting that infant regeneration is common. Alexander argues that God would not do this often, as it could give the impression that grace is natural. Rather they suggest the possibility. Alexander sums up:

> Although the grace of God may be communicated to a human soul at any period of its existence in this world, yet the fact manifestly is, that very few are renewed before the exercise of reason commences; and not many in early childhood.

He confesses how perplexing childhood piety can be. Some, despite every advantage, show little sign of godliness when young. Others appear quite pious in their early years but it may come to nothing. Personally, I have come across very few reliable cases of people claiming to be born again under the age of ten. Even when people say that they were it is worth remembering with Kuyper how in the natural world we remember nothing of our birth and only actually recall certain things from early childhood.

In other ages, especially where deaths among children were more common, early conversions happened perhaps more often. Spurgeon was aware of many examples. An eyewitness to the 1904 revival in Rhos, North Wales, told many years later how 'there were no special meetings for young people; they all came to the adult meetings.' He says that children as young as 'six and eight years of age were talking about Jesus' making their teachers weep 'as they overheard the children's conversations'. Not all were converted but some were.

Edwards' *Narrative of surprising conversions* famously records the testimony of four-year-old Phebe Bartlet who showed genuine evidence of conversion. Further back again, in 1672, James Janeway published his *Token for children* detailing the conversions and other experiences of about twenty pious children. Interestingly, he mentions at least one child, Anne Lane, who he believed was 'sanctified from the very womb'. A very popular book, Janeway's *Token* was supplemented in 1700 by Cotton Mather who added another ten cases from New England, including that of Priscilla Thornton who, in her final throes and full of faith, asks:

Mother, why do you weep when I am well in my soul? Will you mourn when I am so full of joy? I pray, rejoice with me.

Janeway says fairly,

Are the souls of your children of no value? They are not too little to die, they are not too little to go to hell, they are not too little to serve their great Master, nor too little to go to heaven!

Spurgeon, like Alexander, wisely warns against unrealistic expectations of any who profess faith at a young age but we must not make the mistake of supposing that children, even the very young, are incapable of receiving new birth.

Perhaps most come to new birth sometime between their early teens and late twenties, but there are plenty of examples of people being reborn at various stages in life and just as there is no cut-off point in early life so there seems to be none at the latter end either.

The story has often been told of the conversion of a New England farmer called Luke Short. Short was converted, quite amazingly, in his *hundredth* year. Apparently he was sat in a field contemplating his end one day and recalled a striking sermon he had heard some eighty-five years before as a fifteen-year-old in Dartmouth, England. The preacher had been the Puritan John Flavel. His text was 'If any man love not the Lord Jesus Christ, let him be Anathema, Maranatha' (1 Corinthians 16:22, AV). Short lived a further sixteen years after his conversion and despite his sinful past became a faithful member of the Congregationalist Church meeting in Middleborough, Massachusetts. Such a late conversion is undoubtedly very rare. Conversions of people in their seventies, eighties and nineties are equally unusual, but they do happen and we should not be surprised when they occur.

As for 'deathbed conversions', again they do happen. Boswell quotes Samuel Johnson's approbation of the epitaph of an outwardly wicked man:

Between the stirrup and the ground
I mercy sought — and mercy found.

John Newton claimed to have seen more than one such conversion and thought there were probably many instances. While checking this chapter for the last time a friend shared how her brother-in-law's mother had been born again shortly before her death after a lifetime of unbelief and unhappiness. Of course, it is fair to say that it is very difficult to be sure when such professions are genuine. Sometimes a reported deathbed conversion cannot even be verified. There is only one eleventh-hour conversion in the Bible — that of the dying thief. As J. C. Ryle put it: 'One thief was saved that no sinner might despair, but only one, that no sinner might presume.'

The vigour factor

Alexander claims that just as people are born physically weak or strong in constitution, so there seems to be a corresponding variety spiritually: 'There is as much difference in the original vigour of spiritual as of natural life.'

Someone like a Saul of Tarsus comes tearing from the blocks like an athlete set on winning the race, while others seem to struggle right from the beginning. Similarly, just as in the natural world some are born in weakness yet soon thrive well enough, while others are vigorous at birth but struggle thereafter, so in the spiritual world we see the same phenomena. This is something that John Bunyan brings out well with the variety of characters who reach the Celestial City in his *Pilgrim's Progress*. Among those who safely cross the river are not only characters like Honest, Valiant and Steadfast, but others such as Ready to halt, Despondency and Feeble-mind too. It is good to keep such variety in mind when we are weighing up whether we ourselves, or someone else, is regenerate or not.

The knowledge factor

Alexander also points out how a person's knowledge can affect the way that he understands his experience and how he expresses himself. He imagines two newly regenerated individuals — one well taught in Christian things, one very ignorant. Although we may well come away with quite different impressions of the two, the fact is that both have been reborn. Given the right instruction, who can say which one will flourish best in the future?

I remember in my college days a friend who professed to have been born again six years previously at an evangelistic outreach for children but who had not been allowed to attend church on a regular basis. Determined to make the most of her time in university, she attended church and the Christian Union activities with great enthusiasm but, because her family had given her no encouragement in Christian things, she did not even know where to find the readings in her Bible. The Holy Spirit uses means and without the required knowledge a person may appear, in such rare circumstances, to be unconverted even though they were born again some time before. No doubt there are people in, say, China today who have been born again yet, because of their difficult circumstances, they may well appear to be quite unorthodox in their views.

This fact must not be abused, but out of ignorance a person may live contrary to certain Christian teachings and practices and may appear not to be born again when in fact he is. Of course, if he is genuinely reborn that will show itself when his errors are pointed out.

Far from arguing against religious instruction and faithful teaching prior to conversion, this observation argues rather in its favour. The better instructed people are, the better they will be able to discern their standing before God and benefit from being reborn.

Alexander takes opportunity to warn against the stereotyping of testimonies in churches. His cautions against receiving Christians into churches by testimony are unwarranted but his warnings are worth heeding nevertheless. It is very easy for a pattern to develop so that new converts expect that they have to fit a certain paradigm when they make their statements to the leaders or before the church. For some, the temptation may be to sound different to everyone else. There is merit in his observation that 'a frequent and indiscriminate disclosure of these secret things of the heart is attended with many evils'. How easily pride and hypocrisy can be unintentionally encouraged.

> The better instructed people are, the better they will be able to discern their standing before God and benefit from being reborn.

Alexander raises the interesting question of how little knowledge one needs in order to be regenerated. One can imagine a person becoming a Christian despite many deficiencies in their knowledge. Certainly, if what we profess to know about Christian things is true, it will help us and even where, for some reason, knowledge is very meagre, regeneration may still occur.

111

The temperament factor

The other main factor discussed by Alexander is temperament. We said earlier that regeneration involves a change of nature or quality not of being or substance. A person's attitudes will be profoundly affected by the new birth but his fundamental personality will remain the same. There are, to use outmoded Medieval terms, the sanguine, the choleric, the melancholic, the phlegmatic; or in more modern terms — architects, champions, crafters, composers, counsellors, field marshals, healers, inspectors, inventors, masterminds, performers, promoters, protectors, providers, supervisors and teachers! Some are placid, others more excitable; some pessimistic, some optimistic. There are insider or outsider types, clubbable or reclusive, leaders or followers, introverts or extroverts.

Such factors cannot decide whether a person is born again but they can affect his perceptions of regeneration and the way he handles it. Even when people use exactly the same words, the meaning can greatly differ in reality. Some people are very easily moved, others are not. For one person to say he was profoundly moved and filled with joy may mean something quite different to what another means, even though they say the same thing.

Alexander goes on to speak of those who have a 'morbid' temperament. He then discusses melancholy or depression and the effect it has particularly on those who are under conviction of sin. He rightly refutes the idea, sometimes expressed, that Christian experience is likely to make a person more prone to depression or other mental disorders. There are plenty of examples of Christians who struggled with depression but they were generally helped rather than hindered by the fact that they were born again. Think of Luther, Cowper, Brainerd and Spurgeon as examples.

Examples

It would be odd to close without citing at least some examples of regeneration. Even the great John Owen cannot discuss regeneration without introducing a biographical element. He considers the story of Augustine.

Under deep conviction, Augustine had become a rather miserable young man in his early thirties. Then one day, as he lay crying over his sins in a garden near Milan, he heard a voice telling him to 'take up and read'.

He arose and read at random from Scripture, alighting on Romans 13:13-14:

> Let us behave decently, as in the daytime, not in orgies and drunkenness, not in sexual immorality and debauchery, not in dissension and jealousy. Rather, clothe yourselves with the Lord Jesus Christ, and do not think about how to gratify the desires of the sinful nature.

As soon as he had read the sentence he felt a light breaking in on him and he felt safe. He was born again and began to serve the Lord with great energy, penning works such as his *Confessions* and *The City of God* that continue to be a blessing to God's people to this day.

Martin Luther once described his conversion, which came after many a long struggle with sin and confusion and unbelief, in these terms:

> Now I felt as though I had been immediately born anew and had entered Paradise itself. From that moment the face of Scripture as a whole became clear to me ... The expression 'the righteousness of God' which I so much hated before now became dear and precious — my darling and comforting word.

C. H. Spurgeon was another miserable young person. One Sunday morning in January 1850 he set off to church in the snow and came to a Primitive Methodist Chapel in Colchester where a small congregation had gathered. The regular minister was unable to reach the place and so, in Spurgeon's words, 'a plain, unlettered, lay preacher ... stood up in the pulpit, and gave out' his text, Isaiah 45:22:

> Look unto me, and be ye saved, all the ends of the earth: for I am God, and there is none else.

Spurgeon says,

> He had not much to say, thank God, for that compelled him to keep on repeating his text, and there was nothing needed — by me, at any rate — except his text. I remember how he said, It is Christ that speaks. I am in the garden in an agony, pouring out my soul unto death; I am on the tree, dying for sinners; look unto Me!

114

Look unto Me! that is all you have to do. A child can look. One who is almost an idiot can look. However weak, or however poor, a man may be, he can look; and if he looks, the promise is that he shall live. Then, stopping, he pointed to where I was sitting under the gallery, and he said, that young man there looks very miserable. I expect I did, for that is how I felt. Then he said, there is no hope for you young man, or any chance of getting rid of your sin, but by LOOKING TO JESUS; and he shouted, as I think only a Primitive Methodist can, Look! Look, young man! LOOK NOW! And I *did* look; and when they sang a hallelujah before they went home, in their own earnest way, I am sure I joined in it. It happened to be a day when the snow was lying deep, and more was falling; so, as I went home, those words of David kept ringing through my heart, *Wash me and I shall be whiter than snow*; and it seemed as if all nature was in accord with that blessed deliverance from sin which I had found in a single moment by looking to Jesus.

In more recent times C. S. Lewis wrote in *Surprised by joy:*

I know very well when, but hardly how, the final step was taken. I was driven to Whipsnade one sunny morning. When we set out I did not believe that Jesus Christ is the Son of God, and when we reached the zoo I did. Yet I had not exactly spent the journey in thought. Nor in great emotion.

As for myself, I was at a Friday night evangelistic meeting for young people in my home town. It was the early seventies so my hair would have been touching the panda collar on my Ben Sherman shirt. I would have worn flares, stack heel lace-ups and possibly a tank top knitted by my mum. It was a long time ago! After a sausage and chips meal, we sat and listened to the visiting speaker. It was springtime and I remember sneezing a lot with hay fever but I was still gripped.

I do not recall very much of what the speaker actually said, though I am sure he urged us all to trust in the Lord Jesus. Afterwards he gave us something to read and the minister of the church urged me to look at John 3, which I probably did. I certainly prayed, confessing what a rotten sinner I was and asking that I might be born again. I do not remember church the day after next but certainly the matter was still on my mind when I headed for school the following Monday. I was determined to let others know that I was now trusting in Christ. I was not brought up in a Christian home and so for me this change was quite a dramatic one in many ways.

Just over a year later I was baptized by immersion at the same chapel where I had been converted. Ten years after that, after time away studying in Aberystwyth and London, I was ordained to the Christian ministry in the very same place.

Since then my sister and mother and my oldest son have been born again, as well as several others who I have known personally. It is my great longing that there may be many more.

So we have considered something of the diversity of experience that those who are born again can know in terms of age, vigour, knowledge, temperament and other factors. Again we recognize God's sovereign right to save whom he will, when he will, as he will.

9.
How can you tell
it has happened?

'Everyone who believes that Jesus is the Christ is born of God, and everyone who loves the father loves his child as well'
(1 John 5:1).

Here we look at characteristics of the twice born, such as shunning the habit of careless sin, believing only Christ can save, being holy, loving other believers and persisting in Christian living despite the world.

From what we have said, it is clear that being born again is something inward. It happens in the heart so, by definition, you cannot directly observe it. The question arises, therefore, as to how we can tell if a person has been born again or not. J. C. Ryle rightly comments that 'It is a most important thing to have a clear and distinct view on this part of the subject we are considering.' We are going to be judged one day and as everything hangs on the hinge of new birth we must be absolutely clear about whether we have been born again or not.

An obvious way of tackling the question is to say that just as we know that we have been born because we exhibit signs of life (movement, respiration, growth, etc.) so, in a similar way, we can know we have been born again by looking for signs of life. Question: How do I know if I have been reborn? Answer: Am I living as a Christian? Archibald Alexander says that as 'spiritual life is progressive in its nature' then 'habitual growth in grace is the best evidence of its reality'.

George Swinnock takes a story from Tacitus about a father telling his son that he had a book with a list of soldiers who were going to be especially honoured but he is not allowed to tell his son if his name is there. However, he is able to tell him the sort of qualities that those listed there share. In a similar way we do not know the names in the Lamb's Book of Life but we do know the qualities found in such people.

We need to take care here as there are some things that we might be tempted to see as decisive evidences that are either irrelevant or, at best, inconclusive. We can speak of a number of indefinite evidences. For example, having a certain amount of knowledge about Christian things cannot be conclusive. Nor can good deeds or high morals be decisive factors. We may possess certain gifts, such as an ability to pray or preach, but of themselves they prove nothing. Think only of Judas Iscariot to see that. King Herod (in some versions of Mark 6:20) 'did many things' in response to John's preaching and King Ahab even 'tore his clothes, put on sackcloth and fasted ... and went around meekly' (1 Kings 21:27). However, neither was converted. Being baptized, attending communion or joining a good church are not conclusive either, nor is being fully involved in Christian activities such as worship and evangelism.

In his work on the religious affections, Jonathan Edwards lists some twelve things that fail to prove that a person is a Christian. Strength and liveliness, certain bodily effects, great warmth and readiness to speak of Christianity, spontaneous emotions, ability to relate our experiences to certain Scriptures, evidence of love, variety, comfort and joy, spending much time in the outward duties of worship, praising God with our mouths, supposed assurance or the ability to give a moving account of our experience — none of these things individually or altogether can in themselves prove one way or the other whether we are converted.

You may have a conscience that agrees that you are a Christian. You may have a tender heart, a hatred of sin and a love for God's Word. These are excellent things but again they cannot *prove* regeneration. Having a reputation for being a Christian is not the same as being born again. No amount of zeal, persecution or patience under trial can absolutely prove anything. Even strong hopes of heaven and willingness to die for Christ are inconclusive. In Matthew 7:22-23 Jesus speaks these sobering words:

> Many will say to me on that day, 'Lord, Lord, did we not prophesy in your name, and in your name drive out demons and perform many miracles?' Then I will tell them plainly, 'I never knew you. Away from me, you evildoers!'

Having a reputation for being a Christian is not the same as being born again.

119

There is such a thing as a mere form of godliness (2 Timothy 3:5).

Such considerations are rather daunting at first sight. What then *can* prove that I have been born again? Thankfully, there is in the New Testament a little book written with the very purpose of providing us with conclusive evidence. I refer to 1 John and its tests of life. John says there plainly (5:13),

> I write these things to you who believe in the name of the Son of God so that you may know that you have eternal life.

We can divide things in various ways but basically there are five tests of life in the book, five marks of those who are truly born again.

They avoid the habit of thoughtlessly sinning

In 3:9, John says,

> No one who is born of God will continue to sin, because God's seed remains in him; he cannot go on sinning, because he has been born of God.

In 5:18 he adds:

> We know that anyone born of God does not continue to sin; the one who was born of God keeps him safe, and the evil one cannot harm him.

How can you tell it has happened?

John is not suggesting some sort of perfection in the reborn sinner. However, after his second birth, sin will no longer be his natural inclination. He has come to God and the devil cannot have a field day with him as he once did. Scottish preacher 'Rabbi' Duncan put it this way:

> The new creature does not sin, but the complex man, in whom the new and old man is, he sins. These two, while inconsistent and contrary, are not incompatible.

Benjamin Beddome wrote:

> The principle of grace will always be rising up against sin, and at length will triumph over it.

The regenerate man has broken with sin and will no longer live in it as he once did. The born-again sinner sins, but he can never be content in his sins again.

He prays:

> Dear Saviour, let us now begin
> To trust and love thy word,
> And by forsaking ev'ry sin,
> Prove we are born of God.

Does it bother you when you sin? If not, then you are certainly not born again.

They believe that Jesus Christ alone can save

In 5:1a we read the simple statement that 'Everyone who believes that Jesus is the Christ is born of God.' Faith is, perhaps, the very first evidence of regeneration. The one who is born again puts his confidence only in the mediation of Christ. In Acts 16:14 we read of Lydia that 'The Lord opened her heart to respond to Paul's message.' It was the opening of her heart that led to the response of faith in Jesus as her Mediator.

Jesus of Nazareth is the one and only Messiah. Anyone can make that statement, of course, but to truly believe it for ourselves we need the inward work of the Holy Spirit in regeneration. Do you believe that Jesus Christ is the only one who can save you, and are you trusting in him alone? If not, then you cannot be regenerate.

They live a life of holiness

1 John 2:29 says, 'If you know that he is righteous, you know that everyone who does what is right has been born of him.' This is similar to our first point. We are not saved by what we do but if we have really been transformed within, it will show itself outwardly in the way we live. Like David we may sometimes fall but like him we will consider all God's precepts right and we will 'hate every wrong path' (Psalm 119:128). We will live holy lives; lives shaped by the dictates of God's Word. Does holiness mark your life increasingly? We can sometimes be poor judges of this and it is possible to backslide, of course, but the general trend in the life of the true believer will be

toward increasing holiness. Where there is no sign of this, that person has reason to doubt whether he has been born from above.

Thomas Watson tells of a born-again man being approached by the Corinthian courtesan Lais, a woman with whom he had once willingly consorted. He says to her, 'But I am not the same man'. He understood the new birth well.

Holiness is something else that marks out the reborn believer. It is not exactly the same as morality. A truly holy person recognizes that God's Law is spiritual so it requires perfect conformity of attitude as well as action. The holy man thinks, feels, wills and acts in line with the Word from a motive of love for God and desire for his glory. His sanctified affections are the source of his Spirit-aided efforts to obey. Morality, on the other hand, has its spring in mere natural affection. It seeks only outward conformity to the letter of the law from an ultimately self-interested spirit.

They have a special love for all true disciples of Christ

Genuine love for fellow Christians is another sure sign of regeneration. This comes out in several places. For example, 3:14-15:

> We know that we have passed from death to life, because we love our brothers. Anyone who does not love remains in death. Anyone who hates his brother is a murderer, and you know that no murderer has eternal life in him.

> **If you have known new birth then you will have a genuine love for all true believers.**

In 4:7 John exhorts: 'Dear friends, let us love one another, for love comes from God.' Our love needs encouraging. The truth, however, is that 'Everyone who loves has been born of God and knows God,' or as it is in 5:1b: 'Everyone who loves the father loves his child as well.'

Peter makes a similar point in 1 Peter 1:22-23 when he links 'sincere love for your brothers' and loving 'one another deeply, from the heart' with being 'born again, not of perishable seed, but of imperishable, through the living and enduring word of God'. Paul writes to the Thessalonians, interestingly, 'Now about brotherly love we do not need to write to you, for you yourselves have been taught by God to love each other' (1 Thessalonians 4:9).

Samuel J. Stone reminds us that what is true of us as individuals is true of the whole church.

She is his new creation
By water and the Word.

Do you love your brothers and sisters in Christ? We know that believers are full of imperfections and sometimes they are hard to love, but if you have known new birth then you will have a genuine love for all true believers. 'By this all men will know that you are my disciples, if you love one another' (John 13:35).

They persevere in Christian living in spite of the world

Finally, in 1 John 5:4 we read how God's commands are not burdensome to the reborn sinner 'for everyone born of God overcomes [or, is overcoming] the world'. The truly regenerate are able to some extent to withstand the pressures of the world and to overcome temptation and to serve the Lord. This is possible, the verse concludes, because we now have the gift of faith: 'This is the victory that has overcome the world, even our faith.' And so the truly regenerate person learns to mourn, as if he did not; to be happy, as if he were not. He buys things as if they were not his to keep and uses the things of the world, as if not engrossed in them (see 1 Corinthians 7:30-31). In Beddome's words:

> The world is not the object of his pursuit, nor, as far as he acts in character, had he any anxious or disquieting cares about it. He neither inordinately thirsts after it, nor is much concerned to part with it.

For he sees that this world in its present form is passing away.

It is clear from these verses that everyone who is born again will be converted. There is no suggestion in the Bible that a person may somehow be born again and yet not go on to be converted or that there may be a prolonged gap between these two events.

Here are the sorts of conclusive evidence we need to seek for if we wish to be sure that we are truly born again. The list is not exhaustive. We could easily add other criteria. 'Like newborn babies' we will 'crave pure spiritual milk, so that by

125

it' we 'may grow up in' our salvation (1 Peter 2:2). There will be love for our enemies, true joy in God, desire for his glory, submission to his will, a great sense of thankfulness and a sense of the leading of God's Spirit. In Galatians 5:22-23 Paul lists the fruit of the Spirit. Clearly if these things — love, joy, peace, patience, kindness, goodness, faithfulness, gentleness and self-control — are not in evidence to some extent, then why would we suppose the Spirit has changed us? At the same time, increasing illumination is bound to bring home to us how sinful we are and increasing conviction and sensitivity to sin is bound to be a feature in the life of any person who has really experienced the second birth. In the eighteenth century the Anglican evangelical Charles Simeon once remarked that 'the very first and indispensable sign of regeneration is self-loathing and abhorrence'.

We have mentioned Edwards' *Religious affections*. He lists fourteen signs of true affection arising from a genuine new birth. Alexander says that one could easily halve the number to make it more manageable. After speaking of the root, object and basis of true spiritual affections, he discusses spiritual understanding and humility, a changed nature, Christlikeness, tenderness, balance, desire for holiness and good Christian practice.

The Saint's cordial of 1629 by Puritan Richard Sibbes included a fascinating sermon, 'The touchstone of regeneration'. It examined the issue using Isaiah 11:6-9:

The wolf will live with the lamb, the leopard will lie down with the goat, the calf and the lion and the yearling together; and a little child will lead them. The cow will feed with the bear, their young will lie down together, and the lion will eat straw like the ox. The infant will play near the hole of the cobra, and the young child put his hand into the viper's nest. They will neither harm nor destroy on all my holy mountain, for the earth will be full of the knowledge of the LORD as the waters cover the sea.

Sibbes says it is 'an eminent and infallible mark of regeneration to have the violence and fierceness of our cruel nature taken away'.

He goes on to identify harmlessness, sociableness, constancy, inwardness, tractableness (willingness to yield to God) and simplicity as marks of the regenerate. He then uses this for consolation and exhortation.

In two chapters on the subject, another Puritan, George Swinnock, focuses on holiness, growth in grace and trying to win others to Christ. 'Grace, like fire,' he says, on the latter point, 'cannot be hid.'

John Wesley's sermon on 'the marks of the new birth' just mentions faith, hope and love. Faith and love we have mentioned. As for hope, Peter says that 'new birth' is 'into a living hope' (1 Peter 1:3). Wesley ties this to the presence of the Spirit of adoption witnessing with our spirits that we are God's children. To have Christ in you is, of course, the hope of glory (Colossians 1:27).

Two dangers confront us in this area — on one hand, wrong-headed presumption, and on the other, needless despair. It is God's will that every newborn Christian should know that he has entered God's kingdom. Nevertheless, not all have the

> It is God's will that every newborn Christian should know that he has entered God's kingdom.

same level of assurance about this. It is better that we enter heaven doubting our new birth than that we go to hell falsely assuming we have been born again.

God does want us to be assured and by his grace a full exposure to his Word, regular self-examination and a constant looking to him are excellent means for keeping us from unwarranted confidence or an unnecessary lack of assurance.

Pink gives a useful set of questions to ask ourselves. 'Let each one of us test and search himself in the presence of God by these questions,' he urges. We paraphrase:

How does my heart stand with regard to sin? Am I deeply humbled and full of godly sorrow after I've given in to it? Do I genuinely hate it?

Is my conscience tender, so that I'm disturbed even by so-called little sins? Does it humble me when I see pride and self-will in my heart? Do I detest the wickedness of my heart?

Is my desire for the world dead and am I alive to God? What fills my mind when I'm at leisure?

Do I enjoy praying and reading the Bible or do I find it irksome and a burden? Can I honestly say, 'How sweet are your words to my taste, sweeter than honey to my mouth!' (Psalm 119:103)?

How can you tell it has happened?

Is communion with God my highest joy? Is his glory the most important thing in all the world to me?

Against this rightly high view of what the new-born Christian should expect to see in himself we place these heartening words of Alexander who recognizes that although 'the deep-rooted principle of sin has received a deadly wound in regeneration' still 'the carnal life lingers, and sometimes struggles with great force to recover the mastery of the soul'. Although sin appeared to be dead, it clearly is not. It lies 'concealed in the depths of a deceitful heart'. When the believer discovers 'the strength of his corruptions' and 'the feebleness of his graces' it can discourage him. He greatly fears overthrow, but as he looks to the Lord who is faithful, despite defeats as well as victories, he comes to some sort of equilibrium and is enabled to keep in step with the Spirit who has begun this good work in him and will complete it.

As we have said, temperament and other factors come into this. For some the glass is always half empty, for others it is always half full. When we engage in self-examination we must allow for such factors. Always, however, there will be an antipathy to careless sin, faith in Christ alone, holy living, love for fellow believers and persistence in Christian living regardless of the world.

10.
Where does it fit in?

*'One of those listening was a woman named Lydia, a dealer in
purple cloth from the city of Thyatira, who was a worshipper of
God. The Lord opened her heart to respond to Paul's message'*
(Acts 16:14).

Having considered regeneration at some length we here
come to ask where we should place it in our thinking about
the way God saves people. Where does it fit theologically? We
now look at new birth in relation to predestination, conversion,
justification, sanctification and baptism.

In order to understand a statement, it is often important to
have it in context. Only in that way can it be properly analysed.
When studying a period of history it is often helpful to know
what happened immediately before and after the years in view.
With most topics there is some use in seeking to understand
where it fits into the overall scheme. This is certainly true when
it comes to theological matters such as regeneration.

When theological writers look at the subject of being born again they usually come to it in their studies of the work of the Holy Spirit (pneumatology) and particularly in their study of how God saves people (soteriology). When a person becomes a Christian, the Spirit does many things in that person's life and it is useful to try and set out in some sort of order what those things are. The term 'order of salvation' has often been used for this or, more poetically, 'the golden chain'.

Therefore we want now to consider where regeneration is to be placed in the plan of salvation and where it comes in the experience of the individual believer.

Regeneration and predestination

In Romans 8:29-30 Paul says,

> For those God foreknew he also predestined to be conformed to the likeness of his Son, that he might be the firstborn among many brothers. And those he predestined, he also called; those he called, he also justified; those he justified, he also glorified.

This verse contains a golden chain assuring us that God works all things together for the good of his children in such a way that they will certainly be saved. There are inevitable links that ensure this. All who are foreknown by God are 'predestined to be conformed to the likeness of his Son'. All who are predestined are called. All who are called are justified. All who are justified will go to heaven.

It is clear then that all who are truly regenerate are first foreknown and predestined. God's foreknowledge is best understood as the setting of his love on certain individuals, before the creation of the world, in eternity. Having loved them before time, God predestined that these same people should one day come to resemble his Son Jesus Christ. This begins, of course, when a person is born again.

It is important that we remember that behind regeneration is election and predestination. No one can know whether God has chosen and predestined him by enquiring into the records of heaven but we do know that all who are foreknown and predestined will certainly be called and, although Paul does not mention it specifically here, born again. It is regeneration and what follows on that reveals whether a person has been chosen by God.

Regeneration and effective calling

In the gospel there is a general call that goes out to all people to repent and to trust in Christ. We can also speak of an effectual or effective call. This is a special, gracious, inward and irresistible call from God by which sinners are made willing to come to Christ.

Becoming a Christian is not about volunteering. God the Father effectively calls his people to himself as he chooses. The general call may be heard many times before there is an inward and effective call. God's Word is the outward means and the Spirit works within, enabling the person to hear and then to respond. Those who hear this call pass from the state of sin and death in which we all are by nature, to a state

132

of grace and salvation through Jesus Christ.

Some want to say that the effective call is the same as regeneration. Others see it as preceding regeneration. Still others say it follows on. Abraham Kuyper talks about regeneration as *the implanting of the life principle.* He suggests that it is followed by *the keeping of the implanted principle of life* and that the internal call often only comes later. This attempt to reflect on Scripture in the light of the Christian experience of those who grow up in Christian homes is interesting but surely untenable in the light of Scripture.

> Those who hear this call pass from the state of sin and death ... to a state of grace and salvation through Jesus Christ.

Though, logically, regeneration must precede the internal call, as the call cannot be heard without a renewal, it is best to see regeneration and the call as simultaneous in time. We are describing what is almost the same thing but in two different ways. The bestowing of life and the bestowing of the ability to respond to the gospel are almost identical. Being born again leads to a life of obedient holiness and the parallel effective call leads to fellowship with Christ and holy living. One obvious difference would be that one is conscious of effectual calling but not of new birth.

Regeneration and conversion

When we use the word regeneration in its narrower sense, as we have in this book, it is important to distinguish it carefully from conversion. Archibald Alexander does not think the difference so important (probably because he has experience in mind rather than theology), but he does say that regeneration (the communication of spiritual life) is God's act, and conversion (turning from sin to God) is our act and a consequence of the divine influence.

Early Southern Baptist James P. Boyce was a student of Alexander's. Unsurprised at how people fail to distinguish the two he also calls regeneration 'the work of God, changing the heart of man by his sovereign will, while conversion is that act of man turning towards God with the new inclination thus given to his heart'.

A catechism by Boyce's fellow Baptist John A. Broadus reads: 'Does faith come before the new birth?' 'No, it is the new heart that truly repents and believes.'

'Saving belief of the gospel' was for nineteenth-century Presbyterian R. L. Dabney 'the first and most uniform action of the new-born soul'.

In more recent times, R. C. Sproul has spoken of the dramatic moment in his life when, to his surprise, he saw a professor write on a chalkboard 'regeneration precedes faith'. It was a shock to the system for the young seminarian who, until then, had thought in terms of faith leading to rebirth and justification. Going back to his Bible he found that the professor was right. Not only that, but he discovered how men like Augustine, Luther, Calvin, Edwards and Whitefield had taught the same thing.

Conversion consists of repentance and faith and it is being born again that makes these two possible. It is not that by repenting and trusting in Christ we are born again, but that by being born again we are enabled to repent and trust in Christ. Kuyper says that some old Scottish theologians would speak of the implanting of the faith-faculty (regeneration) followed by faith-exercise and faith-power. Without the faculty, the exercise of faith and its power cannot be known.

Turning to Acts 16:14 once again, it was as Lydia listened to Paul preaching that, 'The Lord opened her heart to respond to Paul's message.' It was when the Lord worked in her heart to open it that she was able to respond to the message with faith and repentance.

We are almost never, if ever, able to detect any delay between regeneration and conversion but it is important to recognize that it is new birth that leads to repentance and faith and not the other way round. One writer compares the difference between actually turning on a tap and the moment the water begins to come out. We do not normally distinguish these two as (in most cases) one follows so closely on the other, but there is a logical difference, just as there is between being born again and conversion itself.

It is important to keep the two separate in our minds because, as we have said, whereas new birth is monergistic — something God does alone — conversion is synergistic — it involves our co-operation with God. There are plenty of exhortations in the New Testament to repent and to believe, but none to be born again. As we have said, what Jesus says in John 3 is not a command. Faith and repentance are themselves God's gifts, of course, as 2 Timothy 2:25 and Ephesians 2:8-9 make clear. They are impossible without him. Nevertheless, at the same time, they are things that men themselves do.

For Puritan Thomas Adams:

Repentance is a change of the mind and regeneration is a change of the man.

Using statements by Charnock and A. A. Hodge, we can say of regeneration and conversion that one is like the cause, the other like the effect; one is God's act, one our act; we are unconscious of one, conscious of the other; in one power is conferred, in the other it is exercised; one is an unrepeatable, single act, and the other is constant and progressive. Kuyper says that,

> the first *conscious* and comparatively co-operative act of man is always *preceded* by the original act of God, planting in him the first principle of a new life, under which act man is totally *passive* and *unconscious*.

In a helpful little book, *Spiritual birthline: understanding how we experience the new birth*, Stephen Smallman presents a diagram paralleling physical and spiritual birth. In the top line is conception, pregnancy, delivery and growth, which he matches, in the bottom line, against regeneration, effectual calling, conversion and sanctification. Conversion is faith and repentance which corresponds with the way, at delivery, a baby cries. Conversion then is not the beginning of life but, as it were, when the baby cries for the first time. That fits with a similar analogy used by Erroll Hulse:

> Spiritual life is the consequence of spiritual quickening. The baby cries because it is born; it is not born because it cries.

Regeneration and justification

We have already alluded to the difference between justification and new birth. As sinners, we have two basic problems confronting us. On one hand, there is our guilt; on the other, there is our pollution. It is a little like the problem of how to help a man who has been in trouble with the police many times before and has broken the law once again. He needs not only to atone for the crimes he has already committed but a way needs to be found to stop him engaging in criminal activity again in the future.

Our problem is both our relationship with God and our sinful nature and character. We need not only to find pardon from God but also to be renewed within so that we do not go on sinning in the way we have in the past. We need to be cleansed both from sin's guilt and from sin's power.

When God restores a sinner to himself, he forgives that person so that they are pardoned, all their sins are cancelled and their guilt is removed for ever. He imputes righteousness to them instead of guilt. This is justification. It is concerned with a change in one's legal standing before God. By means of justifying grace, God the Judge makes that person right before him. The sinner is clothed, as it were, in the robe of Christ's perfect righteousness. Justification is the opposite of condemnation. Though every sinner deserves to be condemned those who trust in Christ are found righteous through him.

> **We need to be cleansed both from sin's guilt and from sin's power.**

Justification is obtained when, in Pink's words, 'having been brought to lie in the dust as an empty-handed beggar, faith is enabled to lay hold of Christ'. It is as the repenting sinner believes that he receives a full and free pardon.

God also puts the Holy Spirit within and makes a person holy, a man of God. This comes through regeneration, sanctification and glorification. It is at the new birth that 'sin receives its death-wound, though not its death'. The other two cannot follow without it.

Justification and regeneration, then, are inseparable but distinct. Both are absolutely necessary. Without a pardon we have no right to heaven, without the change we would not be fit for heaven.

Regeneration and adoption

More than that, God also legally *adopts* each believer as his son and heir. Calvin says, 'The Spirit of regeneration is the seal of adoption.' Charnock speaks of adoption as giving us the *privilege* of sons, and of regeneration giving us the *nature* of sons. We cannot explore it here, but this is adoption. Normally a father will not legally adopt someone who is his son by birth anyway. Yet, there is a sense in which God does that for his people.

The other need is to be made into a new person who wants to obey God. Those who are justified receive the Spirit of God and are born again; they then go on to live a holy life. Justification and adoption occur outside of a man and affect his standing before God. New birth, like sanctification, happens within a man's heart and affects his whole life.

God does these two things then. In Charles Wesley's words, 'he breaks the power of cancelled sin' and 'he sets the prisoner free'.

Regeneration and sanctification

Sanctification is to do with being or becoming holy. We can speak of two sorts — definitive and progressive. One is like a full stop, the other like a line steadily ascending. The moment a person becomes a Christian there is a sense in which he is holy as he is now set apart to God. See 1 Corinthians 6:11: 'But you were washed, you were sanctified, you were justified in the name of the Lord Jesus Christ and by the Spirit of our God.' Hebrews 10:10 teaches the same thing. However, there is also an ongoing or progressive sanctification that results in increasing holiness. That is how Hebrews 10:14 can speak of Jesus, 'by one sacrifice' making 'perfect for ever those who are being made holy'.

If progressive sanctification is a line or a river, regeneration is a full stop or a fountain that coincides with definitive or initial sanctification. The new birth is the 'first gleam of dawn' and sanctification is the 'shining ever brighter till the full light of day' (see Proverbs 4:18). In 2 Thessalonians 2:13 Paul speaks of believers being chosen 'to be saved through the sanctifying work of the Spirit and through belief in the truth', but he could equally have spoken of new birth and faith.

Regeneration is the point where the line of progressive or ongoing sanctification begins. Anthony Hoekema says, 'The two are related to each other as initial newness and progressive newness.' He points out, by way of example, how one of the things that should happen when a person is born again is that he should love his brother (see 1 Peter 1:22-23):

> Now that you have purified yourselves by obeying the truth so that you have sincere love for your brothers, love one another deeply, from the heart. For you have been born again, not of perishable seed, but of imperishable, through the living and enduring word of God.

New birth has led to purity and sincere love for fellow Christians. This must now be capitalized upon by seeking to 'love one another deeply, from the heart'.

Samuel J. Stone gets the balance right in this prayer:

> Author of our new creation,
> Giver of the second birth,
> May Thy ceaseless renovation
> Cleanse our souls from stains of earth,
> And our bodies ever be
> Holy temples meet for Thee.

Regeneration and baptism

In Romans 6:1-11 Paul speaks of baptism and associates it with the new spiritual life that Christians have. He says that all 'who were baptized into Christ Jesus were baptized into his death' and concludes:

We were therefore buried with him through baptism into death in order that, just as Christ was raised from the dead through the glory of the Father, we too may live a new life. If we have been united with him like this in his death, we will certainly also be united with him in his resurrection. For we know that our old self was crucified with him so that the body of sin might be done away with, that we should no longer be slaves to sin.

He concludes: 'count yourselves dead to sin but alive to God in Christ Jesus'.

Similarly, in Colossians 2:11-12 he says,

In him you were also circumcised, in the putting off of the sinful nature, not with a circumcision done by the hands of men but with the circumcision done by Christ, having been buried with him in baptism and raised with him through your faith in the power of God, who raised him from the dead.

As we have suggested, Paul has Spirit baptism in mind in such places but water baptism is no doubt also in the background. We made clear back in chapter 1 that baptism and regeneration must not be thought of as the same thing. However, in the sense that it is something done to you by another, once and for all, as a symbol of union with Christ, it is a very good picture of new birth.

Whatever view we take of the subjects (infants or professing believers) and mode (sprinkling, pouring or immersion) of water baptism, it is important that we do not suppose that it can of itself bring about or promote new birth. Rather, water baptism is a sign and seal of regeneration. Those who baptize infants are anticipating something they hope will happen to the one being baptized. Those who baptize believers do so on the basis that the washing of new birth has already taken place in the life of the one passing through the waters.

- Are you baptized and born again? This is how it should be.
- Are you unbaptized and not reborn? Being baptized cannot guarantee new birth.
- Are you born again but not baptized? All those who are regenerate should be baptized.
- Are you baptized but not regenerate? Again we want to urge you pray that you will be born again.

We have sought to state where regeneration comes in the chain of salvation, considering new birth in relation to predestination, conversion, justification, sanctification and baptism. There is some room for debate here but we trust that the basic contours outlined have a biblical foundation. As for regeneration and glorification, we will turn to these in the next chapter.

11.
What are
its cosmic dimensions?

'Jesus said to them, "I tell you the truth, at the renewal of all things, when the Son of Man sits on his glorious throne, you who have followed me will also sit on twelve thrones, judging the twelve tribes of Israel"'
(Matthew 19:28).

This chapter considers some of the larger implications of the Bible's teaching on regeneration, especially the new heavens and the new earth.

We have already pointed out that although the idea of regeneration occurs in many places in the Bible the actual word itself appears in only two places in the New Testament. Paul uses the word in Titus 3:5 where he speaks of God having saved Christians 'through the washing of rebirth and renewal [or regeneration] by the Holy Spirit'. When Jesus uses the word, he uses it in quite a different way.

Matthew 19:28

In Matthew 19:28 Jesus says to his disciples that one day they will 'sit on twelve thrones, judging the twelve tribes of Israel'. This will be when Jesus himself 'sits on his glorious throne'. Jesus also refers to this coming period as the time of 'the renewal [or regeneration] of all things'.

When people use the word 'regeneration' in a non-theological way they often speak of 'neighbourhood regeneration', 'social regeneration' or 'community regeneration'. We have been concentrating throughout this book, however, on the spiritual regeneration or new birth of the individual. Sometimes true Christians are criticized for what at times appears to be a rather narrow concentration on the individual. Such criticisms may be deserved at times, but certainly the Bible itself cannot be accused of a narrowness of that sort. It shows a concern throughout not just for individuals but for the whole cosmos. As Peter Toon has written, the truth is,

> that personal regeneration is part of a cosmic activity by God which involves the whole created order and provides the Christian community with wonderful promises on which to rest.

In Matthew 19:28, Jesus is referring to the end of this world and the bringing in of the new age. It is the time of judgement for this world and the time when he will bring in new heavens and a new earth and rejuvenate all things.

He uses pictures to describe such a time. He speaks, for example, of a great banquet with many guests, a wedding banquet with roast 'oxen and fattened cattle', of feasting 'with Abraham, Isaac and Jacob in the kingdom of heaven' (Luke 14:16-24; Matthew 22:1-14; 8:11). A new order of things is coming and it is those who have first been born again who will enter that kingdom of gladness.

Apostolic teaching

This vision of the future is found in the writings of the apostles too. Peter speaks in Acts 3:19-21 not only of sins being 'wiped out, that times of refreshing may come from the Lord' but also of God sending 'the Christ, who has been appointed for you — even Jesus' who will 'remain in heaven until the time comes for God to restore everything, as he promised long ago through his holy prophets'.

We have spoken of the restorative powers of the new birth. As our souls have been restored and refreshed already so there will come a time when all things are going to be restored or regenerated. We most often speak of this in terms of glorification although it is as much an entire or completed sanctification (just as regeneration is an initial sanctification), or, in terms of regeneration, the external and universal regeneration that follows internal and personal new birth.

> A new order of things is coming and it is those who have first been born again who will enter that kingdom of gladness.

In 2 Peter 3:10-13 Peter, echoing Jesus' own words in Matthew 24:29, 35, says,

> But the day of the Lord will come like a thief. The heavens will disappear with a roar; the elements will be destroyed by fire, and the earth and everything in it will be laid bare … That day will bring about the destruction of the heavens by fire, and the elements will melt in the heat.

In the light of this, he urges believers to 'live holy and godly lives as you look forward to the day of God and speed its coming'. Those who have been born again are those who, having been transformed within, look forward 'in keeping with his promise' to 'a new heaven and a new earth, the home of righteousness'.

In Romans 8:19-24 Paul similarly looks forward to the time when the creation 'will be liberated from its bondage to decay and brought into the glorious freedom of the children of God'. Presently it 'waits in eager expectation for the sons of God to be revealed' and is 'subjected to frustration, not by its own choice, but by the will of the one who subjected it'. It is, as it were, 'groaning as in the pains of childbirth right up to the present time' because it too awaits regeneration. He describes Christians as those 'who have the firstfruits of the Spirit' — the regeneration of creation has begun in us. We 'groan inwardly as we wait eagerly for our adoption as sons, the redemption of our bodies' that is to come.

To put it in the simplest terms, it is not only individuals who need to be born again but also the whole of creation. This will happen when Christ returns to judge the world.

What are its cosmic dimensions?

The Book of Revelation, of course, gives a wonderful picture of the coming glory. John begins chapter 21 by saying,

> Then I saw a new heaven and a new earth, for the first heaven and the first earth had passed away, and there was no longer any sea. I saw the Holy City, the new Jerusalem, coming down out of heaven from God, prepared as a bride beautifully dressed for her husband. And I heard a loud voice from the throne saying, 'Now the dwelling of God is with men, and he will live with them. They will be his people, and God himself will be with them and be their God. He will wipe every tear from their eyes. There will be no more death or mourning or crying or pain, for the old order of things has passed away'

(vv. 1-4).

The verses that follow fill out this picture. The one seated on the throne says, 'I am making everything new!' He is the 'Beginning and the End' who enables his people to inherit all this and to escape the second death of hell. The work, as we have seen, begins on earth with the regeneration of men, women and children, and ends in heaven with the bringing in of the eternal glory of the new heavens and the new earth.

The Christian then is one who lives in the 'now' and the 'not yet'. Already he has been born again and is a new creation. He knows that there is more ahead, however. With creation itself he stands on tiptoes looking forward to a glorious future when Christ will make all things new. With Robert Lowry he can say,

My life flows on in endless song;
Above earth's lamentation
I hear the sweet though far off hymn
That hails a new creation:
Through all the tumult and the strife
I hear the music ringing;
It finds an echo in my soul —
How can I keep from singing?

He prays with Horatius Bonar:

Come, and make all things new,
Build up this ruined earth;
Restore our faded Paradise,
Creation's second birth.

We have briefly looked at some of the larger implications of Scripture teaching on the new birth, especially the new heavens and the new earth. No doubt much more could be said. We have merely attempted to broach the subject.

12.
A final plea

'Jesus said to them, "I tell you the truth, at the renewal of all things, when the Son of Man sits on his glorious throne, you who have followed me will also sit on twelve thrones, judging the twelve tribes of Israel"'
(Matthew 19:28).

In this closing chapter we make a final plea, first to any reader who is not born again, looking at some objections often made, then to those who are.

Someone once said that every person is either born twice and dies once or is born once and dies twice. That is to say, they are either born, then born again and although they die, they go on to heaven to share in God's glory there; or they are born, then die and face the fiery lake of burning sulphur that is the second death (Revelation 21:8).

This testimony is true and most sobering. We have all been born once and, clearly, we will all die once — perhaps sooner than we think. The question then is clear. Are you born again or will you know the second death?

We have explored the subject of regeneration quite thoroughly and, if you have been following, your understanding of it should by now be very clear. What a cruel irony, then, if having read this far, you should prove not to be born again. That would be a tragedy of eternal proportions.

We have considered the marks of regeneration in a previous chapter. In this final chapter I want simply to plead with anyone who has read thus far and yet has not been born again.

One of the problems some raise is that if regeneration is God's work then there is nothing they can do to bring it about. If God saves, he saves; if he does not, there is nothing that can be done. Similar things are said about predestination and justification.

In an address on the subject, the nineteenth-century American theologian W. G. T. Shedd points out that all such arguments come from unconvinced sinners and are no different to all their other empty arguments — that they are not helpless sinners, that they do not deserve endless punishment, so why can they not be redeemed except by vicarious atonement, etc. 'Such opinions as these', he says, 'must be given up, and scriptural views must he adopted, before the Holy Spirit will create the new heart.'

Mere orthodoxy will not save anyone either. If you do not reflect on the truth, if you make no effort to acknowledge your guilt and danger but live on in thoughtlessness and pleasure, what good can it do? You need to see how the law of God applies to you as much as to anyone else. You must become what Shedd and others call 'an anxious inquirer'.

Questions about man's relation to regeneration will give no serious trouble to any convicted man; to anyone who honestly acknowledges that he is a guilty and helpless sinner, and seeks deliverance from the guilt and bondage of sin. The questions will then answer themselves.

Shedd goes on to answer three objections made to the idea of praying for new birth.

The prayer of the unregenerate is sinful

The first objection is that if you are not born again then your prayer is sinful. This proves too much. On this basis the unregenerate can do nothing. Listening to preaching or reading a book is sinful too, yet the Bible never suggests that those who are not reborn should not listen to preaching.

Yes, the thinking of a wicked man, like his driving, his eating and everything else he does, is sinful. None of his actions spring from real love to God so cannot truly be good. Nevertheless, some things are better than others. Specifically, some are better introductions to God's work of regeneration than others. Going to a church where God's Word is faithfully preached is more likely to lead to new birth than going to a sporting event or a play. Praying is more likely to bring blessing than not praying or doing something else.

Shedd notes Puritan John Owen's distinction regarding a deed being good in regard to its matter but sinful in regard to its form. An example would be someone hearing God's Word who is not born again. An example of a deed where matter and form are both bad would be an unregenerate man seeking mere worldly pleasure on the Lord's Day. To follow the first example is far preferable to the second. One is positively commanded by God, the other positively forbidden.

To argue that someone who is not born again cannot pray for regenerating grace because of the sin in his soul is wrong. If it was true, the same argument could be applied to a born-again person praying for holiness. The prayers even of those who are born again are mixed with sin. If you cannot pray until rebirth because your prayers are sinful then you cannot really pray until you are perfectly holy either. If the presence of sin is a reason for not praying in one case, it is in the other.

Therefore we urge anyone who is not born again to pray for it to happen, not because new birth is obtained by prayer as such but because there is no better way to prepare for it. It is better to pray than do nothing. The prayer of the unregenerate is marred by sin, but not necessarily any more than any other prayers.

Only the prayer of faith is certainly granted

Another argument says that given that faith follows new birth, it is impossible to pray for regeneration with faith. If a prayer lacks faith there can be no guarantee of it being answered, so why pray?

Again the logic is faulty. It is true that there is no cast-iron guarantee that the prayers of those who are not born again will be heard, but, as Shedd says, that is no reason not to offer a prayer that will still *probably* be granted. God encourages such prayers and urges us to believe they are answered. The fact that there is no guarantee of a response does not mean there is no hope. The prayers of those who are not born again do not deserve answers but that is no proof that God will not answer.

> The prayers of those who are not born again do not deserve answers but that is no proof that God will not answer.

There are two big differences between the prayers of the regenerate and the unregenerate. First, when those who are born again pray for holiness, God is bound to answer because he has committed himself to this by a promise. On the other hand, he has not promised to answer every prayer for regeneration. In one case there is a covenant; in the other, there is not. God has promised to sanctify every believer who asks for it. He has not promised regeneration to every convicted sinner who seeks it. Regeneration conforms to God's purposes in election. Election cannot depend on a human act such as prayer. Therefore, the convicted sinner's prayer cannot *definitely* secure regeneration in the way that a believer's prayer will *definitely* lead to sanctification.

Whenever a person seeks regenerating grace, he must accept God's right to answer as he pleases. Our attitude should be as Paul commends (2 Timothy 2:25). We must 'hope that God will grant ... repentance leading ... to a knowledge of the truth'; but there is no guarantee. These words are worth bearing in mind too:

> Who knows? God may yet relent and with compassion turn from his fierce anger so that we will not perish
>
> (Jonah 3:9).

153

Rend your heart and not your garments. Return to the
LORD your God, for he is gracious and compassionate,
slow to anger and abounding in love, and he relents
from sending calamity. Who knows? He may turn and
have pity and leave behind a blessing — grain offerings
and drink offerings for the LORD your God

(Joel 2:13-14).

Like the leper, come to Jesus and say, 'If you are willing, you
can make me clean,' (Mark 1:40).

What about 'Everyone who calls on the name of the LORD
will be saved' (Joel 2:32; Acts 2:21; Romans 10:13)? This either
refers to the prayer of someone under conviction and should be
seen as a general statement that God will hear, or it refers to the
prayer of a regenerate person for sanctification. Whoever calls
on the name of the Lord in faith and repentance will be saved.

The other big difference is that a prayer for sanctification
is a part of the sanctification process while a prayer for
regeneration is not part of regeneration. If prayer was a means
God had appointed for new birth it would certainly secure its
end, but it is an appointed precursor not a means, so we have
to say it will *probably* not *certainly* be answered.

God has not committed himself to hear the prayer of every
convicted sinner without exception, but that does not mean
such prayers are useless. Thousands and millions have prayed
and been heard. Since the cross, it has been his general policy
to hear such prayers. Such prayers we can say are *likely* to
succeed. God is merciful. He will surely hear.

To say that God never grants the prayers of an unregenerate
man is untrue. Such people have called on God to spare their

lives and he has heard (see Psalm 107:10-14). From a sense of danger, a fear of wrath, people under conviction have prayed to be saved from hell and God has heard. He answers not because the prayer is holy or deserves an answer but because blessing is needed and he is merciful to sinners in Christ.

Such prayers are not only likely to be answered but also have a good effect on the one who prays. No one can study God's Word and be illumined by it without having his sense of danger awakened so that he prays in that light. Even a prayer that is only a cry of fear and lacks son-like trust and humble submission is useful. The prayer's very defects prepare the person for new birth. It shows him how much he needs to be transformed.

In distress he asks for a new heart. No answer comes at first. His heart is disappointed. Perhaps it is made more bitter and rebellious. By this experience, the Spirit discloses more and more the animosity of a man's unbelieving mind and the weakness of his self-enslaved will. He sees increasingly his need of new birth.

The *Westminster Confession* is surely right to say that 'Prayer, being one special part of religious worship, is required by God of all men.' The Bible gives every encouragement to pray for regenerating grace. Everyone without exception is urged to seek it, just as they are urged to listen to God's Word. See, for example, Psalms 65:2; 86:5; 145:18; Isaiah 55:6; Luke 11:14; Acts 9:11; Romans 10:12; 1 Timothy 2:8. These and similar texts invite and command men universally and indiscriminately to ask God for the Spirit in any of his operations, as the first and best of his gifts.

Regeneration is a sovereign act of God in line with election but it is encouraging for sinners and those who preach to them to remember that regenerating grace is commonly preceded by seeking God's face. Indeed, this is the norm in this New Testament period. Those who read and meditate on God's Word are usually enlightened by the Spirit, perhaps in the very act of reading, hearing or meditating. 'While Peter was still speaking these words, the Holy Spirit came on all who heard the message' (Acts 10:44).

If a person asks for new birth he may well be born again in the very act of praying. Conviction of guilt and danger, a sense of sin and a realization of one's utter inability to do anything good are all useful. This is the breaking up of the fallow ground (Jeremiah 4:3; Hosea 10:12). The grace of conviction is often followed by the grace of regeneration. Nevertheless, the wind does indeed blow where it pleases. Sovereign grace is all. The unsaved person must take great care, then. To suppress conviction can mean the withdrawal of all grace. God is sovereign and is free to do as he chooses. Without minimizing his patience and tolerance we must say how dreadful it is to be left to our own self-will.

Shedd says preachers are like farmers, sea traders or manufacturers who sow grain, send out ships or erect factories on the basis of probable success. Salvation is highly likely for anyone who earnestly and diligently uses the means of grace. Conviction often leads to new birth. We must work on that basis.

To pray for new birth is to delay faith and repentance

Sinners are commanded to immediately believe on Christ and turn from sin with godly sorrow. To pray for new birth, it is suggested, is to waste time. It is an excuse for putting things off. In fact to pray for regeneration is to pray that the Spirit will work immediately on the heart and instantly renew and incline the will.

> ...to pray for regeneration is to pray that the Spirit will work immediately on the heart and instantly renew and incline the will.

If it was suggested that prayer was a means of regeneration then there would be force in the argument. If a person is told to pray that God will grant new birth at some future point by this means the charge would make sense. But if a person who truly prays for regenerating grace despairs of all means and is not putting things off, then he clearly seeks immediate change. He is imploring God, 'who said, "Let light shine out of darkness," made his light shine in our hearts to give us the light of the knowledge of the glory of God in the face of Christ' (2 Corinthians 4:6).

Consequently, prayer for regenerating grace is an evidence that a convicted person has come to realize that all ordinary means of grace are inadequate to revive his soul and renew it so that it is righteous. It is when he realizes that nothing else will do that he begs God for an immediate and instant work in his soul. The prayer for regenerating grace is the most energetic and pressing act that the sinner can perform. It is not procrastination at all.

Prayer for the instantaneous gift of regenerating grace fits in with the gospel call to immediate faith and repentance. They follow regeneration and so to pray for instant regeneration is, virtually, to pray for instant faith and repentance. To ask for regenerating grace is to make every effort to enter through the narrow door (Luke 13:24).

A plea to those who are not born again

George Swinnock is keen to help people to regeneration and spends well over half his book *The door of salvation opened by the key of regeneration* on this. With him we urge you to a serious consideration of the new birth and what it does; to get to know the steps the Spirit takes to renew souls and to be willing to submit to his workings and to make a serious and constant use of the means of grace. Keep praying, reading and watching, always remembering that the blessing comes from God.

Swinnock also deals with objections similar to those considered above. People make the excuse that if the new birth is something that God does, then there is nothing they can do. All they can do, they argue, is to fold their arms and wait to see if God makes them into a new creature. But they forget that all the while, far from folding their arms, they are, by nature, constantly raising their fists to God in defiance. The truth is that people do not accept their utter dependence on God anywhere near enough. If you truly believed there was nothing you could do, you would be crying to God night and day for mercy.

Dabney uses the illustration of a man whose house is burning down. He is upstairs gathering his treasures. The flames are licking higher and higher but he believes that he can escape when he chooses. Under that delusion he is moment by moment putting himself in greater and greater danger.

Look and see — the staircase has already burned away. Soon the whole house will be gone. Run to the window and see that your only hope is to drop all your treasures and jump now. We say to you with Dabney, 'Cry to God.' Cry out, 'Save, Lord, or I perish.'

> It is the very thing, the only thing, which a helpless sinner, who is guilty for his very helplessness, should do.

A plea to those who are born again

Finally, what if we are born again? Firstly, we must give God all the glory. Everything we do, even eating and drinking, should be for his praise. 1 Corinthians 4:7 asks:

> For who makes you different from anyone else? What do you have that you did not receive? And if you did receive it, why do you boast as though you did not?

What thankful people we should be if we really have been born again. 'Light is sweet, and it pleases the eyes to see the sun' (Ecclesiastes 11:7). If that is true on the physical plane, how much more on the spiritual. We should be thankful both for physical and spiritual life.

Secondly, what are we doing to win others to Christ? If we truly believe that there is no entry to heaven without new birth, then what are we doing to make others aware of the fact? What are we doing to see that others are born again?

This consideration should affect the way we live. Our lives must be structured in a way that will not drive people away from Christ but that will make the teaching about the Saviour attractive.

It should affect our prayers. We cannot fully understand the complexities of how prayer makes a difference but we know that people are born again when they and others pray. People prayed that we would be born again and we were. We in turn also ought to pray for others to receive the second birth.

> ...we should be as eager for new births as most women are to bear their own children.

It should affect the way we speak. As we set Christ apart as Lord in our hearts, we should seize every opportunity to explain the hope we have through new birth. We must be gentle and show respect and keep a clear conscience, of course, but we should be as eager for new births as most women are to bear their own children. Like Paul we should labour until Christ is formed in others (Galatians 4:19).

Spurgeon once pleaded with his congregation to at least do something. It bears repeating:

Oh, my brothers and sisters in Christ, if sinners will be damned, at least let them leap to hell over our bodies. And if they will perish, let them perish with our arms about their knees, imploring them to stop, and not madly to destroy themselves. If hell must be filled, at least let it be filled in the teeth of our exertions, and let not one go there unwarned and unprayed for.

Surely it is an intolerable disgrace to anyone to profess to be a Christian, and have no concern about the souls of others, while they are perishing by millions.

Etiquette nowadays often demands of a Christian that he should not 'intrude' his religion on company. Out with such etiquette! It is the etiquette of hell! True courtesy to my fellow's soul makes me speak to him, if I believe that his soul is in danger.

Brethren, DO something, DO something, DO something! While societies and unions make constitutions, let us win souls. I pray you, be men of action, all of you. Get to work and quit yourselves like men. Old Suvarov's idea of war is mine: 'Forward and strike! No theory! Attack! Form a column! Charge bayonets! Plunge into the centre of the enemy!' Our one aim is to win souls; and this we are not to talk about, but do in the power of God!

We must school and train ourselves to deal personally with the unconverted. We must not excuse ourselves, but force ourselves to the irksome task until it becomes easy.

The unregenerate have many objections. Here we have tried to deal with some of these, urging those still not reborn to seek God. We have also sought to remind those who are born again, including ourselves, of the implications of the fact. Our great longing is that those who are born again may have a good understanding of what that means and that those who are not may come to be regenerated to the glory of God.

Appendix 1

Regeneration under the Law of Moses

The Old Testament passages from Ezekiel and Jeremiah (Ezekiel 35, etc; Jeremiah 31) examined in chapter 4 seem to suggest that regeneration is something for the future. Certainly, it is only when we come to the New Testament era that the Spirit is poured out as he was on the Day of Pentecost. Peter deliberately speaks about it as the fulfilment of the promise in Joel 2.

If by 'regenerate' we mean rightly related to God, enjoying his fellowship and having the Spirit within, then the answer to the question 'Were Old Testament saints regenerate?' is certainly 'Yes'. The Spirit did help them to remain in covenant with God. They knew what it is like to be born again. Nehemiah says to God of the people in the desert, 'You gave your good Spirit to instruct them.' Those who were saved were certainly not saved by the law, any more than those who are saved today. This is why Calvin wrote that those 'under the ancient covenant were gifted and endowed with a spirit of regeneration'.

It is misleading then for the Dallas professor J. Dwight Pentecost to suggest that 'the fact of the new birth (regeneration) had not been revealed in the Old Testament'. It is better to say with Roy L. Aldritch of Detroit that 'The new birth is characteristic of every period since the fall, even though this doctrine is not as clearly revealed in the Old Testament as in the New.'

A. W. Pink has written of the Old Testament period:

> The Spirit prompted true prayer, inspired spiritual worship, produced his fruit in the lives of believers then (see Zech 4:6) as much as he does now. We have 'the *same* Spirit of faith' (2 Cor 4:13) as they had. All the spiritual good which has ever been wrought in and through men must be ascribed unto the Holy Spirit. The Spirit was given to the Old Testament saints *prospectively*, as pardon of sin was given — in view of the satisfaction which Christ was to render unto God.

John Piper has helpfully written that 'all the saints of the Old Testament who trusted God and followed his ways in the obedience of faith were born again by the Spirit and indwelt by the Spirit'. Piper cites Psalm 139 as evidence that they had the Spirit's constant presence.

It is under the covenant of grace that a person is saved but old covenant believers were blessed in old covenant ways and new covenant believers in new covenant ways. Under the new covenant, God works in a much more extensive and powerful way. Jeremiah 31:34 says, 'They will *all* know me, from the least of them to the greatest.' The focus on Christ, who was active in the Old Testament but has now appeared in these last days, is more obvious too. Something similar can be said of the Holy Spirit. When a person is born again, it is because the Spirit is at work within and they are beginning to take on the likeness of Christ. Strictly speaking, this is something that happens to New Testament believers not Old Testament ones. Just as we would probably want to avoid the phrase 'Old Testament Christian' so we normally do not speak of Old Testament believers as being born again. At the same time, to quote Calvin again, we remember that 'the new covenant so flowed from the old, that it was almost the same in substance, while distinguished in form'. Certainly any suggestion that Old Testament believers did not have faith in Christ or the indwelling of the Spirit must be avoided.

When Jesus speaks to Nicodemus about being born again then he is speaking chiefly of spiritual renewal, but he is also directing him to the blessings of the new covenant that he was soon going to bring in through his death and resurrection and the sending of the Spirit.

Appendix 2

Sample historic confessions or creeds that support a monergistic view of regeneration

From the Canons of Orange (AD 529)

Canon 6: If anyone says that God has mercy upon us when, apart from his grace, we believe, will, desire, strive, labour, pray, watch, study, seek, ask, or knock, but does not confess that it is by the infusion and inspiration of the Holy Spirit within us that we have the faith, the will, or the strength to do all these things as we ought; or if anyone makes the assistance of grace depend on the humility or obedience of man and does not agree that it is a gift of grace itself that we are obedient and humble, he contradicts the apostle who says, 'What have you that you did not receive?' (1 Corinthians 4:7), and, 'But by the grace of God I am what I am' (1 Corinthians 15:10).

Canon 7: If anyone affirms that we can form any right opinion or make any right choice which relates to the salvation of eternal life, as is expedient for us, or that we can be saved, that is, assent to the preaching of the gospel through our natural powers without the illumination and inspiration of the Holy Spirit, who makes all men gladly assent to and believe in the truth, he is led astray by a heretical spirit, and does not understand the voice of God who says in the gospel, 'For apart from me you can do nothing' (John 15:5), and the word of the apostle, 'Not that we are competent of ourselves to claim anything as coming from us; our competence is from God' (2 Corinthians 3:5).

From the Canons of Dordt (1618, 1619)

Article 11: The Holy Spirit's work in conversion. Moreover, when God carries out this good pleasure in his chosen ones, or works true conversion in them, he not only sees to it that the gospel is proclaimed to them outwardly, and enlightens their minds powerfully by the Holy Spirit so that they may rightly understand and discern the things of the Spirit of God, but, by the effective operation of the same regenerating Spirit, he also penetrates into the inmost being of man, opens the closed heart, softens the hard heart, and circumcises the heart that is uncircumcised. He infuses new qualities into the will, making the dead will alive, the evil one good, the unwilling one willing, and the stubborn one compliant; he activates and strengthens the will so that, like a good tree, it may be enabled to produce the fruits of good deeds.

Article 12: Regeneration a supernatural work. And this is the regeneration, the new creation, the raising from the dead, and the making alive so clearly proclaimed in the Scriptures, which God works in us without our help. But this certainly does not happen only by outward teaching, by moral persuasion, or by such a way of working that, after God has done his work, it remains in man's power whether or not to be reborn or converted. Rather, it is an entirely supernatural work, one that is at the same time most powerful and most pleasing, a marvellous, hidden, and inexpressible work, which is not lesser than or inferior in power to that of creation or of raising the dead, as Scripture (inspired by the author of this work) teaches. As a result, all those in whose hearts God works in this marvellous way are certainly, unfailingly, and effectively reborn and do actually believe. And then the will, now renewed, is not only activated and motivated by God but in being activated by God is also itself active. For this reason, man himself, by that grace which he has received, is also rightly said to believe and to repent.

Article 14: The way God gives faith. In this way, therefore, faith is a gift of God, not in the sense that it is offered by God for man to choose, but that it is in actual fact bestowed on man, breathed and infused into him. Nor is it a gift in the sense that God bestows only the potential to believe, but then awaits assent — the act of believing — from man's choice; rather, it is a gift in the sense that he who works both willing and acting and, indeed, works all things in all people produces in man both the will to believe and the belief itself.

Article 16: Regeneration's effect. However, just as by the fall man did not cease to be man, endowed with intellect and will, and just as sin, which has spread through the whole human race, did not abolish the nature of the human race but distorted and spiritually killed it, so also this divine grace of regeneration does not act in people as if they were blocks and stones; nor does it abolish the will and its properties or coerce a reluctant will by force, but spiritually revives, heals, reforms, and — in a manner at once pleasing and powerful — bends it back. As a result, a ready and sincere obedience of the Spirit now begins to prevail where before the rebellion and resistance of the flesh were completely dominant. It is in this that the true and spiritual restoration and freedom of our will consists. Thus, if the marvellous Maker of every good thing were not dealing with us, man would have no hope of getting up from his fall by his free choice, by which he plunged himself into ruin when still standing upright.

Article 17: God's use of means in regeneration. Just as the almighty work of God by which he brings forth and sustains our natural life does not rule out but requires the use of means, by which God, according to his infinite wisdom and goodness, has wished to exercise his power, so also the aforementioned supernatural work of God by which he regenerates us in no way rules out or cancels the use of the gospel, which God in his great wisdom has appointed to be the seed of regeneration and the food of the soul. For this reason, the apostles and the teachers who followed them taught the people in a godly manner about this grace of God, to give him the glory and to humble all pride, and yet did not neglect meanwhile to keep the people, by means of the holy admonitions of the gospel, under the administration of the Word, the sacraments, and discipline. So even today it is out of the question that the teachers or those taught in the church should presume to test God by separating what he in his good pleasure has wished to be closely joined together. For grace is bestowed through admonitions, and the more readily we perform our duty, the more lustrous the benefit of God working in us usually is and the better his work advances. To him alone, both for the means and for their saving fruit and effectiveness, all glory is owed for ever. Amen.

From the Westminster Confession of Faith and the 1689 London Baptist Confession of Faith

Chapter 10: Of effectual calling.

1. [All] those whom God hath predestinated unto life, [and those only] he is pleased in his appointed, and accepted time, effectually to call, by his Word and Spirit, out of that state of sin and death in which they are by nature, to grace and salvation by Jesus Christ; enlightening their minds spiritually and savingly to understand the things of God; taking away their heart of stone, and giving unto them a heart of flesh; renewing their wills, and by his almighty power determining them to that which is good, and effectually drawing them to Jesus Christ; yet so as they come most freely, being made willing by his grace (Romans 8:30; 11:7, etc.).

2. This effectual call is of God's free and special grace alone, not from anything at all foreseen in man, [*nor from any power*

or agency in the creature, being wholly passive therein, being dead in sins and trespasses,] until being quickened and renewed by the Holy Spirit; he is thereby enabled to answer this call, and to embrace the grace offered and conveyed in it [*and that by no less power than that which raised up Christ from the dead*].

Confession of Faith of the Calvinistic Methodists of Wales (1823)

26. Of regeneration.

Regeneration consists in a gracious and supernatural change, wrought by the Spirit of God in all those who are saved to eternal life, by making them partakers of the divine nature, which is the principle of a holy life, effectually working in the whole man, and for that reason called 'the new man'. The holy nature received in regeneration acts in all those who are made partakers of it in direct opposition to every form of corruption, and after God who created it. This change produces in the whole man a lively impress of God's holiness, as a child bears the image of his father. God alone is the author of this change. It is generally wrought by means of the word, and is set forth in Scripture under several names; such as quickening, forming Christ in the heart, partaking of the divine nature, and circumcising the heart. This change is wrought in order that men may glorify God by bringing forth the fruits of righteousness, and purifying the soul, so as to be meet to enjoy fellowship with God for ever.

Select bibliography

A number of books have been useful in preparing the foregoing, including several commentaries and systematic theologies. Here we list a selection of books that you may also find useful. There is a very helpful web site with many good articles on this and other subjects at *www.monergism.com*

On regeneration

A. T. B. McGowan
The New Birth
Christian Focus, 1996

J. C. Ryle (1816-1900)
Regeneration
Christian Focus (Christian Heritage series), 2003

George Swinnock (1627-1673)
The door of salvation opened by the key of regeneration
Banner of Truth (Works, Vol. 5)

Peter Toon
Born Again
Baker, 1987

Peter Van Mastricht (1630-1706)
A Treatise on Regeneration
Soli Deo Gloria, 2002

General

Thomas Goodwin (1600-1680)
The Work of the Holy Ghost in our salvation
Banner of Truth (Works, Vol. 6)

Anthony Hoekema (1913-1988)
Saved by Grace
Eerdmans/Paternoster, 1989

John Murray (1898-1975)
Redemption accomplished and applied
Eerdmans, 1955

Edwin H. Palmer (1922-1980)
The Holy Spirit
Presbyterian and Reformed, 1958/1974

Select bibliography

Philip Graham Ryken
The Message of Salvation
Inter-Varsity Press (Bible Speaks Today), 2001